SMALL HABITS TO BIG CHANGES

BECOMING THE BEST VERSION OF YOU

SELINA F.

COPYRIGHT

Copyright © 2020 by Selina F.

All rights reserved. It is not legal to reproduce, duplicate, or transmit any part of this document in either electronic means or in printed format without written permission of the copyright owner except for the use of quotations in a book review.

INTRODUCTION

What makes a successful person different than other people? What is it that enables people like Elon Musk, or Steve Jobs, or Beyoncé to achieve majestic heights of success, when most of us are struggling? What is the common denominator?

The answer is straightforward, really – they do what they need to do when they need to do it. They build a catalog of positive habits that enables them to maximize their potential and defeat the odds every time. They give themselves a reason and, more importantly, a *means* to reach out and touch the stars by developing the right habits to support their goals.

We all want to be happy and successful, but sadly, only a precious few people seem to achieve consistent success in the five critical areas of life: the physical, emotional, social, professional, and financial. It is important to develop habits that result in you being healthy, happy, well connected, satisfied with your career, and financially stable.

Each of these aspects is defined differently by every person, and that is part of the richness of life. But most people fall short of their intentions because they lack the know-how to make every minute of every day count towards their success. They trudge through life, battling with low productivity and negative habits.

This is why you must learn to manage your habits effectively.

Are you a chronic procrastinator? Are you in search of self-discipline? Does your day feel shorter than it actually is? Do you put in your best and still fail to deliver? Do you fail to attain the goals you have set for yourself regularly? Are you that person who goes to bed each night knowing deep inside your heart that you could and should have done more during the day?

If you answered "yes" to any of the questions above then read on. I have written this book to show you how to reach for the greatness that lies within you. It doesn't matter if you have failed so many times in the past that you have lost sight of what success is; this book will help you rediscover the path for you.

The human brain is built to seek out immediate pleasure. Therefore, if you do not create a mental filter to keep you disciplined, you will find yourself forever choosing the easier option at every instance. That is why you end up daydreaming instead of working on that important project. That is why you often choose sleep instead of getting up early to complete your exercise routine. Turn unproductivity into a habit, and you are going to have major big problem on your hands.

Now, how do these negative habits affect our chances of success? Our brain, as the most complex biological structure known to man, is blessed with limitless capacity and unbelievable processing power, but even the brain needs help. When you repeat an action frequently enough, the brain comes to store the process of its execution as a loop that it can put in effect with minimal effort. Think of habits as mental shortcuts/checkpoints that your brain uses to reduce stress.

Your habits can either prove to be your best allies or the greatest threats to your goals. They define you and your limits. When your habits scream commitment, you become known as a committed person. When your habits mark you as being "unproductive," then unproductivity becomes your hallmark. When it comes to habits, it is the little things that matter most: how you eat, the way you think, how you sleep, your attention to time. They all count for a lot in the long run.

This is the lesson that super-successful people learn; they assemble a routine of positive habits that can give them the extra push and lift to succeed. Right from the beginning, Steve Jobs built for himself and his business a culture of excellence and creative freedom. His adherence to his personal principles of comfortability in design and creative freedom within the workforce got him booted out of his own company at first, but undaunted, he soon made a return that took *Apple* right into the stratosphere. In the same way, Cristiano Ronaldo is widely considered to be a model footballer because he made hard work, dedication, and confidence his primary habits. Mark Spitz was the first person to win seven gold medals at one Olympic. How did he do it? He set spectacular goals for himself and proceeded to spend his time in judicious pursuit of those goals. Unshaken by initial failure, he soon found himself at the peak of his profession.

However, it is tempting to live a self-indulgent life shorn of discipline, detailed plans, and commitment to your true goals and life plan. I know because I have been there.

About five years ago, I had extremely low self-esteem, fear of judgements from other people, and unmotivated in all areas of my work. I ate junk food all the time and that slowly turned into my stress-coping mechanism. My days were spent missing deadlines and my nights featured Netflix binges, irregular sleep, and many pints of Ben & Jerry's ice cream. I woke up every day feeling tired and regretful for what I did the previous day, and in dread of what I was about to do the rest of the day. I was a mess!

Luckily for me, I stumbled upon the principles (through hundreds of hours of reading and listening to podcasts from other teachers) that I discuss in this book. Following them gave me the chance to reassert control over my specific habits – and my life in general. In the five years since, I cut out bad habits (like procrastination and stress eating) and almost magically, I seemed to have more time each day. I became debt free for the first time in forever, and I built an online publishing business that earned me a great chunk of side-income. In addition, I picked up a job I like working at, and I get paid for that too. I love to exercise and my BMI has been under 20 since I made these changes. I meditate daily and exercise in the morning; that has given me better control over my emotions. Best of all, I have sufficient time to nurture friendships and spend with my family members. It was hard at first, but by rewiring the neural pathways that control habit formation, I became better in all aspects of my life.

My habits transformation journey led me to the discovery of a phenomenal finding; To truly live the best life, one must enjoy a healthy level or in other words, a state of well-balanced equilibrium in all five golden aspects of life: **financial, physical, emotional, social, and professional/career well-being.**

Written from my past years of long experiments with habit management techniques, this book represents the complete guide for getting rid of negative habits and installing new, positive habits in their place, as a prerequisite for enjoying a new lease on life.

The right habits will change who you think you are as a person. You will move from "procrastination" to "action." You will no longer miss your exercise routines simply because you won't see them as a chore any longer. You will build better working habits because you love what you are doing, and not because you have to do it. Most importantly, you have come to understand how to bring massive improvement to the five major areas of your life (social wellbeing, financial health, physical health, emotional health, and professional development) through transforming your habits.

If you can apply the tips in this book, you will become a better version of yourself. What you need in order to build good habits and eliminate the bad ones is a new mindset, and the information in this book simplifies the process of tweaking your mind and recharging your willpower to succeed. Stocking up on the new, more productive habits that you need depends a lot on your ability to take small steps and remain resolute in your newfound persona.

Why should you read this book? It will teach you

- How habits affect you every day
- How to identify negative habits and the impact they have on your productivity level
- How to achieve an immediate boost in productivity levels
- Why you have been unable to attain the kind of success that your potential and efforts deserve
- The NEXT-LEVEL habits refinement process to help you:

- Take control of your personal finances and never feel stressed about money again
- Improve your physical health (exercise & eating tendencies) and feel more energized than ever
- Take your career progression to the next-level
- Form deeper and more genuine relationships with your family/friends to build the support system you can lean on
- Master your emotions to finally take control of your life, and not let emotions define you

Every one of us is the sum of our most consistent habits. Wouldn't you like to increase your value by improving your habits and routine? This book will provide you with the knowledge and impetus to build the right kind of habits. Two, five, or ten years from now, you will look upon this moment with gratitude if you take the chance to finally get control of your inner psychology now. You should control your habits, and not allow them to control you. This is the time to establish a new routine; do not live your life with your old habits shaping you on autopilot. Reading this book will provide you the reasons and means for becoming a better version of you!

Good luck!

A SMALL GIFT TO MY READERS:
LEARN HOW TO SUPERCHARGE YOUR PRODUCTIVITY!

This 12 page step by step workbook includes:

- 6 in-depth actionable steps to better manage your *energy & time* to fully maximize the quality of your life!
- 2 pages full of life-changing *hacks & tips* to help you stay focus & minimize distractions 24/7.
- done-for-you *productivity tracker template* to help you monitor your progress.

BONUS: get the chance to win **3 copies of the best sellers** in the self-help niche. These books have changed my life in terms of productivity, performance, and happiness!

To receive your free workbook & get the chance to win 3 best-sellers books, please visit:

https://sfpublishing.activehosted.com/f/13

1
THE HABIT LOOP NOBODY EXPLAINED TO YOU

"If you want to lead an extraordinary life, find out what the ordinary do—and don't do it."
— *Tommy Newberry*

In life, we all want success and happiness. We want to be successful at what we do, and we want to be happy while we do it. With humans, the quest to achieve success while remaining happy is second only to the quest for survival. We want to be the best at what we do – a terrific athlete, the great salesman, the loving mother, the dependable friend, the amazing manager – but sadly, we are all built differently, have different sets of habits and operate with unique mindsets. This means that we are going to see the same things differently, come to different conclusions, and act in different ways that are sure to bring different results. Unfortunately, for most people, the results are anything but positive in the long run. Because we currently live in a world that is obsessed with instant gratification and quick fixes, most people aren't considering the long-term aspect. We do things that might feel good to us in the moment, but we lack the perspective of seeing the severe impact years down the road, and this all leads us back to the one thing that matters the most: habit.

Why do people fail? Why have you bought this book? What is the way forward?

Nine times out of ten, the difference in success rate between individuals is down to the discrepancies in their habits and mindsets. Your habits and mindsets determine how much you can do in the pursuit of your goals. The people who succeed possess the right mindset. They pair that with the right set of habits that can give them the lift they require to succeed. So, to rig the odds in your favor, you need to instill the right mindset and then equip yourself with optimal habits that can help you attain success and happiness.

The average individual (who has no control over his habits) is usually trapped in a negative feedback loop that makes it hard for him to produce results consistently. The loop is predicated on how careless habits can become the greatest threats to your wellbeing. To rebuild your mindset and revamp your habits, you need to overhaul this negative feedback loop.

There are four major phases in the LACK - habit loop. In order, these are

- Procrastination
- A lack of discipline
- Inability to achieve goals
- Poor time management

Combined, these four phases twist your mindset and warp your ability to make progress towards success and happiness. Their presence signifies that you already have a catalog of bad habits, and there is no room for progress until you can clear your closet of them. They work together in a negative feedback system that gets stronger with each cycle they complete.

Chronic procrastination can lead to a total breakdown in discipline. The moment you lose discipline and control over your actions and your work process, you fail to complete even your smallest tasks or day-to-day responsibilities. This can lead to mental stress and overwhelm your capacity. The financial, physical, emotional, social, and professional aspects of your existence begin to suffer. One would think that would push the average individual to finally get off this negative cycle. That is the kicker, though – the lack of time, the fact that you are overwhelmed, and the ensuing stress often encourage more procrastination, which leads to further loss of discipline and uncompleted goals. Thus, the negative cycle keeps growing stronger and stronger, and as a result, it genuinely becomes a part of you.

From here on, it becomes virtually impossible for you to enjoy the levels of productivity that your tasks require. You may pick up other negative habits such as addiction to social media or unhealthy eating habits as a compensatory measure. You may begin to neglect your environment and personal space and leave it a mess. With time, this can lead you to the state in which you decided to read this book to find a lasting solution to the frustration brought about by negative habits.

Now, let us look at each of the phases in the LACK habit loop as a prelude to getting rid of it.

Procrastination

The first stage of the LACK loop is procrastination, often aroused from the lack of energy or focus. Procrastination is perhaps the most talked about negative habit today. Many experts have developed plans to battle procrastination and its effects. There are hundreds of hacks and tips floating around the internet that purportedly fix procrastination and improve productivity. But perhaps, that is where the problem is – procrastination is not a problem of productivity. It becomes a problem when procrastination turns into a habit and leads to loss of self-discipline.

I know the vast majority of people think procrastination is important because of its effects on productivity, but we must also understand the root cause of procrastination. Procrastination is an emotional and psychological issue that must be approached as one. You cannot just bluff procrastination away with to-do lists and the loudest alarm clock in the world. You need a shift in mindset to get rid of procrastination.

Let me drop a bombshell here! Occasional procrastination is neither good or bad. In fact, procrastination developed as a protective tool of the brain (and mind). As I have already mentioned in the introduction, the human mind is built to seek out immediate gratification. More importantly, our mind is trained to avoid pain. Let me use an analogy here.

It's as though each one of us has two bulbs in his mind – one that lights up for pleasure and another that signifies pain. Now, almost all the actions we carry out will light up one of these bulbs. Swimming, eating, playing video games, sleeping, etc., can be deemed pleasurable. So they light up the pleasure bulb each time. Tasks that do not provide immediate pleasure or that you consider boring light up the pain bulb. That is why you wince when you remember that you have a presentation to complete at work. That is why you screw up your face at the thought of doing the dishes or mowing the lawn. There is no immediate pleasure to be derived from these actions and they light up the pain bulb in our minds.

You will not complete any task that lights up the pain bulb unless there is greater, immediate punishment for not completing that task then. Instead, your mind will find and substitute that task for something that lights up the pleasure bulb in your mind.

So, you may find it hard to complete that presentation. Instead, you may choose to sleep or catch a game. You may not be particularly interested in sleeping or watching the game at that moment, but it serves as the substitute task that your mind engages to get the pleasure bulb working. You will continue procrastinating about that until "not doing that task" lights up the pain bulb. That may come in the form of a deadline you cannot miss or the realization that you may suffer financial loss if you do not complete the task.

Therefore, you cannot get rid of procrastination until you either tweak that task to light up the pleasure bulb, or you find greater pain in not completing the task at that moment.

In addition, smart people procrastinate the most because they can project the outcome of their actions more clearly. I know the overriding narrative is that smart people work more efficiently and are smart enough not to procrastinate, but this is a wrong belief. In fact, smart people procrastinate because they think ahead more than the average person. A smart person will seek to find a better risk ratio and delay acting until they are sure they are on firm ground. They are attuned to the potential effects of their actions and would rather hold back until they are sure of the potential results these actions will generate. This can form the bedrock of procrastination.

Many of the greatest personalities known in history are adept, chronic procrastinators. You don't need to take my word for it – let me cite some examples.

The Dalai Lama, the head of Tibetan Buddhism and one of the most revered spiritual leaders in the world, has one of the widest reaches in the world. He is typically held up as one of the most upright individuals to ever walk this planet. He is a man with many demands on his time and a fully packed list of tasks to attend to, but even the Dalai Lama has a huge reputation as a procrastinator. Today, he has worked on his procrastination but in his youth, as a student, he was quite the slacker and he always required external help to get motivated.

Bill Clinton, the 42nd president of the United States, was reputed to be lazy, and even described by Time magazine as a frequent "chronic procrastinator". Even Al Gore, his vice-president, alluded to his time management problems back when he was in power.

To say Leonardo da Vinci's impact on the art and science worlds is significant would be an understatement. He created some of the most valuable and notable pieces of art that still survive today. His plans, diagrams, and vision also served as the bedrock for many inventions in the modern world, but was Leonardo an efficient individual, as we have come to think all smart people are? No! It took Leonardo sixteen years to complete the *Mona Lisa,* perhaps the most famous piece of art today. That's not all. He spent thirteen years painting *Virgin on the Rocks* as well. Throughout his life, he was famed for getting into trouble with patrons over missed deadlines and appointments.

These great men (and many more) were no different from you and I. They were just as susceptible to the mental process that throws up procrastination as a defense mechanism. Whenever smart people are faced with difficult choices or situations that hold a lot of risks, they hold off acting until they are sure of what they are getting into, or it becomes too *painful* not to act. Because they are smart enough to understand the potential consequences of what they are doing, they use procrastination as a mental means to hold off until they are sure.

Certain factors can also increase the chances that you will procrastinate instead of acting promptly. They can slow you down by linking the task in front of you with mental pain. It is best to identify within yourself if you have any of these following qualities, and so you can take the right measure to prevent the constant urge to procrastinate.

Perfectionism

Perfectionism is one of the lead causes of unnecessary delays. A perfectionist doesn't want to sail into unknown waters. He wants to be sure of where he is headed and the tools he has in his locker. A perfectionist will wait until the coast is clear before making his attempt. He will not act until the time is right, his tools are right, his rivals are weak, his employees are ready, and he feels the timing is perfect. Therefore, perfectionists get the pain bulb lighted frequently. As a result, they hold off until they are very sure of the right steps to take and how to take them.

Overthinking

If you think heavily, then the chances are that you will always have quite a lot on your mind. This can overwhelm you and force you to delay action. Your own natural curiosity forces you to continue to turn all possible outcomes over in your mind without making an instant decision. In the end, this can push you to put on the brakes and not act.

(Over)Confidence

When you are sure that you can easily handle what is required of you, the task may get relegated to the back burner until it is pressing. Since you do not require further knowledge or skills to complete such tasks, you may subconsciously overlook it for as long as possible.

Addiction to the adrenaline rush

There is no point denying the fact that there is a thrill that comes with rushing against deadlines. It is a glorious feeling to turn in a project or assignment a few minutes before the deadline. Yes, you may make unneeded mistakes, but there is a great feeling, sponsored by adrenaline, that comes with finishing your work with only a few moments to spare. Some people are simply addicted to this feeling, and may find it difficult to complete their actions until deadlines loom large.

In conclusion, procrastination is created out of the mental and psychological need to avoid pain and opt for actions that generate immediate gratification and pleasure. This may even spur you on to heights and limits you couldn't dream of. However, when procrastination becomes a chronic habit and unmanaged, it can lead to undesirable outcomes that will interfere with your goals.

Lack of Discipline

Against the grain of the wider discourse, I have highlighted that procrastination can have benefits. However, when procrastination becomes constant and consistent, it can lead to more significant problems, notably, gradual erosion of discipline.

Paul has just woken up on Sunday morning. The first thing that comes into his mind is the fact that he must turn in his submission for a journal article the next day. However, he has not even started writing. He also remembers that he has not done his laundry for some days now. Of course, he isn't oblivious to the fact that he failed to mow the lawn the previous day as he had planned. The whole house is in disarray, but he cannot bring himself to clean it up. He begins to feel bad about the things he should have done but he still does nothing about them, even now. Instead, two hours later, Paul is seated in front of the TV, a glass of wine in his hand and a bowl of popcorn on the small table in front of him, undecided about where to start his day from.

Does that sound like you? Do you discern a kindred spirit in Paul?

Well, that is a variation of what goes through the mind of every chronic procrastinator. With procrastination comes a loss of discipline that is so often fatal for your ambitions and goals. Why is discipline so important?

Discipline is the ability to stay committed to your goals and plans long after the mood in which you set those goals has passed. Discipline is perhaps the main ingredient in making success. It is the ability to do things you would rather not do, for long-term benefits. It gives you control over your wants, moods, thoughts, and emotions, and ensures that you are ready to make required sacrifices.

To be honest, success is rarely straightforward. In fact, to succeed, you must be willing to do more than or better than most people. You must be ready to forego immediate pleasure and look forward to long-term gains. Therefore, chronic procrastination destroys discipline. It wears off your discipline gradually and causes you to lose focus and the ability to achieve.

One of the distinguishing marks of great people who procrastinate is that they are able to stop procrastinating when it threatens their discipline. That is, they are able to take action when issues threaten to spill out of hand. That explains why Frank Lloyd White was able to draw up a great plan when he was pushed to the wall. The average procrastinator, however, is unable to do this. Procrastination erodes self-discipline.

To most people, self control is hard and punishing. They often liken it to punishing themselves by not doing the things they want to do or ignoring their wants and desires. This mindset, though, is responsible for why most people fail to build sufficient reserves of discipline. Since they have tagged it as "exacting" or "punishing," they find it hard to build the right set of habits that can foster self-discipline.

To build true discipline, you have to understand that long-lasting discipline is only found internally. Discipline represents a balance that you have struck between your wants and your duties, your moods, and your long-term plans. Staying disciplined is a decision that you must make on your own – that's the only way it will work. Other people can provide you with a momentary burst of motivation periodically but their impact will always be temporary. Friends, trainers, family members, and mentors may give you a reason to stay on the course you have plotted but discipline comes from within you – that's why it is called "self-discipline." Self-discipline is immune to interference and is a function of your innermost desire and control. With a self-disciplined mind, it is impossible for changing conditions such as adverse events or the opinions of other people to affect your resolve or make you lose your principles.

In addition, you cannot be disciplined until you define a "WHY" for yourself. If your reason for trying to get disciplined is strong enough, it will be harder for you to quit. For instance, if you want to lose weight, you need to understand why that is important to you. It could be because you have family history of diabetes and you are trying to be proactive or because you want a better physique to live a healthier and longer life, or you want to set a good example to your kids or spouse. If you join a gym for these reasons, you would have greater motivation than an individual who joined only because they want to appear fitter and skinnier for a short-term vacation or special event. What happens after the summer vacation? You will most likely go back to your normal self. You need to have a strong "WHY" behind your goals and the pain of not achieving that goal must be greater than the bad habits you are currently doing. That's the sure way to avoid a loss of discipline.

Discipline is a mental vow between you and your mind. It is easily demonstrable in the way you act. Now, you can never be truly disciplined until you sit down to make that decision. Until you invest mental energy in understanding that discipline offers you a sure path to success, you will always associate discipline with mental pain.

Are you scared of the sacrifice and commitment that comes with discipline? Do you look at disciplined people you know, and think their lives must be very boring? I invite you to come to a new way of looking at discipline. Instead of making it all about your current choices, let it be about the goals and success you want. Robert Kiyosaki said it best, *"Success takes an investment in time, dedication, and sacrifice. This is true education. It is a process."*

To stay disciplined, do not feel as if you are being pushed, make it look like your goals are pulling you onwards. To do this, you need to cultivate the right set of productive habits that will engender discipline in your daily routine. Success or failure are usually not the result of one single, large step or decision. Rather, they are usually the average product of many small steps, thoughts, decisions, and actions taken over a period of time. You can rig the odds in your favor by ensuring that you have the right set of habits.

For people who allow procrastination to become a permanent component of their daily routine, a loss of discipline is almost inevitable. Once you lose discipline, it becomes harder for you to achieve your goals. Think of discipline as that little voice in your head that coaxes the best out of you even in adverse circumstances. Think of discipline in terms of a friendly reminder that you must stay committed to your plan and goals. It is a check-and-balance system designed to help you stay on the path to success.

Failure to achieve Goals

The moment your discipline *fails,* it becomes a herculean task to achieve any of your work, health, or personal goals. Why is this so? Because you lack the courage and will power to keep pushing through. John C. Maxwell said it best, *"Motivation gets you going, but discipline keep you growing."*

Goals require some level of effort and work to make them happen. You cannot set a goal, go to sleep, and expect the goal to be completed. Even more telling, in the quest to complete your goals, a lot of mitigating factors may surface. It could be problems with capital, rivals with the same intent, low revenue, addictions, or a narcissistic partner but most goals have forces trying to prevent you from completing them. When these negative factors come into place, you may get frustrated or lose motivation. You may even quit. In fact, quitting is the most common type of failure. Even if you do not quit formally, you may lose motivation so much that you stop doing the right things. Let us look at New Year Resolutions, for instance. At the start of every new year, people from all over the world draw up goals for the year and make outlandish promises. What becomes of the majority of these goals?

A research study by the University of Scranton reported that only 8% of people fulfill their New Year goals. That is ridiculously low when you look at the verve and gusto with which people proclaim their goals every January. *Strava* went one further in their research and discovered something even more damning. After going through 31.5 million online sources, they reported that most people start reporting failed goals by January 12.

Regardless of other factors, a loss of discipline is the greatest cause of failure to complete your goals and reach your milestones. Nothing can defeat a disciplined individual ready to pay utmost respect to the process of achieving success. History is replete with examples of people who remained disciplined for so long that failure simply ceased to exist as an option.

Colonel Sanders is one such great example.

At the age of 65 years, he received a pension check for $105. Tired of waiting at home to receive the paltry sum, he decided to finally market a chicken recipe that he had developed himself. He went from door to door trying to sell his recipe idea to restaurants and private individuals in the hope that someone might take enough interest to collaborate with him. Five hundred doors later, he still hadn't gotten a single positive reply. Most people would have quit by this stage. After all, nobody really expected a sixty-five years old man to build an empire off a chicken recipe but Colonel Sanders was not "most people." He was a disciplined man who had decided to stick to his guns. He went through more than another five hundred doors before someone took a genuine interest in him. By most accounts, Colonel Sanders pitched his recipe 1008 times before the next person he met decided to take a gamble on the recipe.

Today, every time you look at a KFC logo, Colonel Sanders beams back at you in his iconic white suit. He was the man who got rejected one thousand and eight times before he could reach his goal, but because he refused to give up due to his strong discipline and motivation, success became inevitable.

It is clear to see now how important discipline comes in to place when it comes to helping you achieve your life goals and advancing your life forward. Without discipline, you will always be stuck on the same path, while those with discipline will be able to achieve bigger and better things.

Lack of time

The last stage in the negative habit loop, this phase is characterized by the loss of time during the day due to poor time management skills – bad habits. Suddenly, the day begins to look shorter, there are a million-and-one little things to do, and there is never enough time. When you lose control over your time, life itself descends into chaos. Instead of setting out each day with a clear idea of what the day ahead should look like, you just get swept along by the tides of circumstance and events happening around you.

Rather than live life by your own watch, you get forced to exist within other people's definitions of your time. Each day seems jumbled into the next, with no clear purpose or distinctions and it becomes hard to define your life's worth. It is at this phase that the ill effects of your negative habits kick in.

This is the phase in which most people are trapped, including you. You do not realize it yet but you are trapped in a loop of commitments and tasks that you just do not have enough time for. Bad habits carve out a niche in your life and force you to devote time and scarce resources to maintain them.

Poor time management can cost you in big ways. You may not realize it now but the effect of a poor time-management lifestyle can negatively impact many other areas of your life in different ways.

Mental and physical stress.

It will leave you boxed into tight corners where the only way out is to overexert yourself physically and mentally. Since you do not spend your time judiciously, you will be forced to accomplish more in less time than you would prefer. When you lose control over your time, anxiety is also a common occurrence. Combine anxiety with the sheer amount of ground you will need to make up constantly, and you may understand why poor time management is a potent and valid stressor.

Damage your reputation.

No one wants to work with an unreliable colleague, and that's exactly the reputation poor time management will give you. When you consistently miss appointments and deadlines, you will be under pressure to live up to your potential, and that rarely ends well.

On the other hand, successful time management throughout the day will allow you to

Improve your decision-making process

This is one of the greatest benefits of good time management. You will have more control over the things you choose to do and stay organized all day. With that comes sharper focus as you are able to handle tasks one after the other. You will gain clarity of mind and purpose and be able to concentrate your abilities on one task at a time. Rushed decisions do no one any good. When you make decisions under the pressure of time, there is a higher chance that you may miss an important detail or fail to factor in all requirements and possibilities. When you control your day and time well, though, you will learn to make most decisions long before a deadline is upon you. With that extra bit of time to consider your options, it is highly likely that you will make better choices.

Reduce stress

Stress comes as an admission that you are going beyond your usual limits. Being able to sort out tasks and complete them on time can greatly alleviate the symptoms of stress and anxiety. Better time management will also help you reduce any pending backlogs of work that you need to complete. So, being able to complete them on time will free up more time for you to deal with more work. In the long run, this will greatly reduce the occurrence and effects of stress upon you.

Work better and play harder

Effective time control will help you create more time for yourself. By ensuring that you procrastinate less, good time management skills will give you more time to check out new ideas, do research, and try out new things. That will open up a whole new vista of opportunities to work more efficiently and effectively.

The ill effects of the four phases of the loop result in a loss of control over time. In this state, the seeds of procrastination are sown quicker, and you end up repeating the entire loop.

Procrastination arises from the association (conscious or subconscious) of a task with mental pain. Our brains are built to seek immediate gratification and pleasure. Left to its devices, the brain would always choose the path of least resistance, but that is not always the most beneficial route for us. So you must find a way to rewire that line of thought. For every task you deem too hard or complex, you must find a way to make it light up the pleasure bulb in your brain. When procrastination tarries for too long, it gives way to a loss of discipline.

We are going to come across rough patches in every plan – setbacks that threaten to derail even the best-laid plans, and the only way to go through them is to retain discipline. Discipline is almost a subset of perseverance and motivation. It springs from within and can allow you to operate beyond your limits. However, in people who procrastinate, the level of discipline they can show is severely depleted, so they become more likely to fail in their goals because they cannot offer the minimum requirements in terms of effort.

Losing at your goals or failing in your plans depresses you even further, but this is inevitable for anyone who has lost discipline. Succeeding is as strong a positive emotion as failing is a strong negative emotion. This means that constant failure will set you on edge, cost you optimism, and set you up with too many things to do at once to stay afloat. That will lead to a total loss of control over your time and cause you to lose all sense of direction.

Loss of control over your time means that you will have even less time to complete your tasks – and that is a sure recipe for more procrastination because you now have less time to finish even your smaller jobs. That will make you lose more discipline, fail more often, and lose more time. This way, a vicious cycle that thrives on negative feedback will continue to destroy your ability to make life-changing transformations. Each cycle ends up increasing the effects of the next, and causes an exponential increase in power and impact.

Chapter Summary

Many people are trapped in a vicious habit loop that gradually deprives them of time and the ability to make progress. The key to breaking out of the loop, as I have earlier stated, is to revamp your habits and build new, positive ones. These small habits can cause big changes in your lifestyle and mindset. They can empower you with the framework you need to control your time better and maximize your potential for success. We will be looking at how they do that in subsequent chapters.

2

DEMYSTIFYING HABITS

"Depending on what they are, our habits will either make us or break us. We become what we repeatedly do."
—*Sean Covey*

What are Habits?

The human brain is an efficient, sophisticated biological complex that possess an unbelievable level of processing power. However, even the brain is conscious of the fact that it can get overworked. To save valuable energy, our brain uses habits to run in a semi-autopilot mode from time to time. Therefore, habits represent a form of power-saving shortcuts that our brains employ from time to time.

How much attention do you pay while you brush your teeth? Think about it. You hardly pay any attention at all. Basically, your mind can wander about so many other things while you clean your teeth. You are hardly aware of the different movements needed, yet you clean them very well. This is because cleaning your teeth is a habit that you have formed over time.

The brain has come to understand the processes involved and can effectively run the "brushing" act somewhere in the background while concentrating on other issues.

The same thing applies to driving. The first few times you drove a car, you must have been very conscious of every move you made. You paid attention to how hard you stepped on the gas pedal and watched the lever as you shifted gears. After a few weeks, though, you would have been able to drive without paying as much attention as the first time you tried to drive a car. You probably drive now with little attention paid to the finer details.

Habits extend beyond just daily tasks like brushing your teeth and driving. They are the basis of everything you do – the way you eat, your likes and preferences, and even the way you think. As such, habits are a very important part of our daily activities. Some researchers say about 75% of everything we do daily is due to habits. When you repeat an act long enough, your brain learns to carry it out without much supervision. This can be both a blessing and a curse, depending on the actual habit.

The more times you repeat an action, the easier it is for your brain to store it as a saved reflex that it can easily engage with minimal effort the next time the action is required. As Gretchen Rubin said, "When possible, the brain makes a behavior into a habit, which saves effort and therefore gives us more capacity to deal with complex, novel, or urgent matters." For an act to become a habit, it has to be repeated often or throughout a consistent period of time.

Habits bring rewards, which may turn out to be positive or negative, and drawing from this, we can broadly classify habits into positive and negative habits. Positive habits, as the name implies, bring long-lasting positive effects to your overall well-being in a number of ways. They can improve the quality of life you live, provide you with a productivity boost or simply help you enjoy your relationships better. Positive habits help you build a better mindset and make conscious decisions that can help you maximize your potential. Common examples include eating well, getting adequate rest, meditation, and listening to valuable podcasts. However, positive habits may not always be easy to sustain or develop. I will explain why shortly.

Negative habits, on the other hand, can carve out a niche for themselves in your routine and throw all your efforts at achieving success and personal transformation into the bin. The negative habits are the exact habits that causes the LACK habit loop to run continuously, growing the loop stronger and stronger each time. They make it very hard for you to be productive. In fact, they are the leading cause of failure. They can sabotage your efforts or make it hard for you to make the necessary sacrifices for success. Most of the time, they creep subtly into our routine and continue to grow in strength until they exert a pull on our outlook and ability to make a difference. For most people, it is only at this point that they realize that they have acquired a new negative habit. Some common examples of negative habits include procrastination on big projects, addiction to phone/social media, working on a cluttered desk, overspending, stress eating, and pulling all-nighters.

Rewards Versus Punishments

Why do we retain negative habits for as long as we do, even when it is clear that they are doing us lots of harm and no good? Conversely, why does it seem to be harder to develop and sustain a new, positive habit even when it is obvious that it holds massive life-changing potential?

The answer to this relies heavily on understanding the way our mind is built to work. By default, the human mind seeks instant pleasure at all costs. That is our normal mode – to enjoy every moment as much as possible. This means that unless you show some control, or get forced by the knowledge and threat of punishment, you will always choose an action that promises you immediate rewards.

Sadly, negative habits almost always promise instant rewards and delayed punishment. That is why you may choose to play video games instead of working on the presentation you have. The video game will give you an instant reward, and the consequences of not working when due will come at a later time. Let me use another example.

What does one day of eating burger and fries do to your body? Nothing. Your weight will probably stay around the same, and you would feel the same and look the same. However, if you continue to eat burgers and fries every day for the next six months or two years, you will most likely gain weight. That means there is an immediate reward tied to eating burgers and fries – they taste good at that moment. However, there will be a delayed punishment for eating that kind of food continuously.

On the contrary, positive habits often require you to sacrifice immediate pleasure for delayed rewards. You may need to make a "mental sacrifice" at the moment to reap greater benefits later. Eating healthy foods may not necessarily tickle your palate, for instance. You may find it easier to binge on pizza and soda instead of eating something healthier but less appetizing like chicken breasts and veggies. However, good eating habits require you to let go of the pleasure you would have gotten from the junk foods, for the health benefits you can derive from eating healthily. The same thing applies to working out at the gym. Especially when you are new, exercise routines can be discomforting and outright painful. They can disrupt your mood, cause aches, and force you to take a rest, but in the end they will help you stay fit and build an impressive physique. So, by accepting the instant discomfort or pain by going to the gym and eating healthy foods, you get the delayed pleasure of a nutritious body and an amazing physical appearance.

Understanding Delayed Gratification

The principle of rewards and punishments is the basis for tweaking, building, or deleting any habit. It is also the basis for "Delayed Gratification." What is delayed gratification, and how does it affect your habit-formation mechanism?

Delayed gratification is the ability to make a conscious decision to delay immediate pleasure in exchange for greater rewards in the future. You could call it self-control or the will to hold off the innate craving for immediate pleasure and wait for a far greater return.

For example, partying all night certainly looks more interesting to most students than reading for an exam. However, when you begin to understand the concept and logic behind delayed gratification, you become aware that not reading could cause you to fail, and you are more likely to read than go out and party with your friends. You delay the immediate gratification that may be had from partying to be able to enjoy the greater rewards that excellent grades bring to the table.

For a visual representation of the long term impact of immediate gratification habits vs delayed gratification habits:

*Working out/ reading (top)

*Eating bad /social media (bottom)

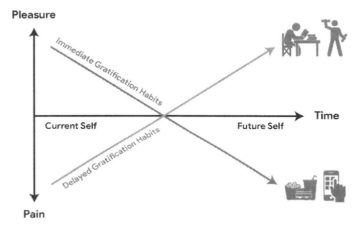

The Marshmallow Test

Between the late 1960s and early 1970s, Walter Mischel ran what eventually became one of the most famous studies on human behavior – the marshmallow test. The study used preschool children from the Stanford University community as the test participants. They were left in a room with a marshmallow in front of them. The researcher told them he was going to leave the room, and gave the children two choices. They could choose to eat the marshmallow in front of them or receive more if they waited until he came back. The researcher then exited the room. The study charted the different kinds of behaviors and actions that each child showed. They all tried to hold off eating the marshmallow for as long as they could. The researcher then recorded how long it took for each child to succumb to the craving.

The research continued to follow the participants over the years. At age fifteen, the results showed that children who could hold off from eating the marshmallow for longer typically recorded higher academic achievement and were able to carry themselves better in social relationships. Conclusively, continued evaluation of the initial participants showed that people who showed delayed gratification better were able to deal with the tendency for anger much more effectively.

Why is Delayed Gratification so Important?

Delayed gratification is a habit on its own. It is the golden habit that you must develop. You must learn to delay immediate pleasure and show some restraint. That will put you in pole position to make better, more productive choices in the most important areas of your life.

In terms of finances, delayed gratification can help you avoid impulsive buying and unnecessary spending. If you have trained yourself to see beyond the immediate pleasure you get from ordering things online or going on a shopping spree, you will be able to save more and provide bigger cash flow for a more salient move in your business.

Delayed gratification can also help you to build better health. It takes some level of self-control to be able to make and stick to healthy choices when it comes to eating. By default, junk food seems to taste better and offer an immediate guarantee of pleasure. However, it can cause you harm in the long run. Being able to delay the gratification you get from it will ensure that you can make smarter choices. Better health is the ultimate gratification in this case.

You can also use delayed gratification to boost your mental health and produce better relationships. How? Every relationship will go through its highs and lows. It is imperative that, regardless of the current phase of your relationship, you learn to overlook things. You can exercise more control and deal with the impulses for anger better by weighing them against the future pleasure that a healthy relationship would bring. Every couple or family gets into fights and arguments, ultimately it comes down to the way you handle these situations that determine the health or wellbeing of these meaningful relationships in your life.

In terms of professional progression, self-control can also be your watchdog. It will ensure you do not cut corners to achieve peak job satisfaction. Delayed gratification also means that you will find it easier to take on new challenges and try your best to succeed at them. It will spur you on to develop and hone your professional skills even better. It may take some initial effort to achieve that, but since you are focused on the larger goal, it will be easier for you to cope with the initial requirements.

Being able to tap into the delayed gratification ethic is no specific guarantee that you will achieve success in life – there are many other factors that come into the equation – but at the very least, it will train you to look at the bigger picture, deal with instant gratification and cravings, and develop the right set of habits that will help lead your way to success.

Chapter Summary

Habits are the brain's answer to multiple, complex tasks. The brain saves repeated actions as action reflexes that can be recalled and engaged whenever needed. However, the brain always favors the path of least resistance and by default, the brain favors negative habits that mostly bring immediate gratification compared to positive habits that may take a bit of delay before its impacts are felt. However, you must master the art of favoring delayed gratification as it brings compounded results in the long run.

3

MAKING THE SWITCH

"You'll never change your life until you change something you do daily. The secret of your success is found in your daily routine."
—*John C. Maxwell*

In the last chapter, I gave you an overview of habits and their importance. I also explained the difference in the impact that positive and negative habits make and listed some of the best habits you should look to develop. The truth, though, is that it is very hard to remove or replace negative habits with positive habits. To stand any chance at all, you must understand the stages we go through to act each time.

The Habit Execution Loop

In Charles Duhigg's book *The Power of Habits*, he introduced to the world this powerful concept of the habit loop. In case you have not heard of this yet, I will briefly explain the meaning and importance behind this cycle as this is extremely valuable to understand the later components that we will cover in the book. Each habit occurs as the culmination of a four-stage process from initial interest to the execution of the act. The four stages are

Trigger

Also known as the cue, the trigger is responsible for initiating the habit. Triggers remind you of the habit and set the ball rolling for the act itself. They can be internal (when they spring from your thoughts) or external. Basically, they fire up the process that ends in the habit. For instance, waking up in the morning can be the trigger for cleaning your teeth and taking your bath. High temperatures can be the trigger for a cool, refreshing bath and nervousness can trigger smoking. When the brain saves a habit, it also saves its trigger. So, the presence of this trigger will cause the brain to initiate the execution of the habit. Our brain is constantly and consistently searching within and without for any trigger it recognizes.

Desire

Triggers alone do not suffice to cause an action to be repeated. Instead, you need some strong motivation for wanting that habit to occur. Your desire has to be compelling enough, or else the brain will shut down that habit at this stage. This stage is mental and internalized – it is the stage at which most failed habits fail. Desire allows you to bring a change to your state of mind. For instance, picking up exercise is not because you like it; it is the desire to build a great body and good health. Yet desire and triggers differ from individual to individual. The same trigger may even cause different reactions. A pair of dice may evoke a strong desire to gamble in a chronic gambler and cause no reaction at all from someone who does not gamble.

Reaction/Response

This is the act itself. After the trigger and desire have been established, you can then perform the habit. It may be an action such as snacking while watching TV. For responses to occur, though, they must still be feasible and capable of delivering a great reward. For instance, you can make a habit out of checking your phone for social media notifications. In this case, the trigger is your notifications popped up, and the desire is that you think you will feel good after checking your phone or you want to be updated of everything that's going on in the world. Then, of course the response is checking your phone.

Reward

This is the feeling that the reaction elicits. It is the goal and focus of the entire loop. The reward can either be positive or negative and is the most important factor in determining if an act would become a habit or not. The reward phase is particularly important because it is the point at which your desire is satisfied. It is at this stage that the brain also traces the entire sequence and stores it as a new habit if you are not used to it.

The four stages in the habit loop can be further grouped into problem and solution phases. The problem phase is composed of the first two stages. Here, the focus is on trying to solve a problem of desire while the solution phase features the reward and reaction stages, where the craving is satisfied.

Every habit follows this loop. Inactivation of any part of the loop makes it impossible to perform the habit. Basically, the rewards that you are used to trigger a desire that allows you to generate a reaction that will bring you the reward. Let us look at a few habits and how the habit loop functions to allow you to execute them.

Trigger	Desire	Response	Reward
You are worried, stressed out or disappointed over a missed goal	You want to reduce stress or escape from work-related worry	You drink excessively and with no limits	You forget about your worries temporarily
You are hungry and tired and so you open the fridge	You want an energy boost	You go ahead and grab an ice cream sandwich	Junk foods become registered as energy-boosting acts for you
You are bored	You want to get rid of boredom	You check your social media feeds and catch up on trends	You get invigorated and more active. Your brain associates social media with relieving boredom
Insomnia or difficulty sleeping	You badly need a distraction to keep your mind off insomnia	You switch on the TV and spend the next few hours watching your favorite show	You do not get to sleep but watching the television takes your mind off the lack of sleep and offers you entertainment in its place

The Role of Dopamine

Dopamine, also known as the pleasure hormone, is responsible for the "good feeling" that accompany the reward phase. Dopamine release is behind the thrill as you puff on a cigarette and the way you feel when the effects of regular exercise start to kick in. However, there is such a thing as dopamine addiction. Dopamine addiction occurs when you are very used to the thrill that dopamine provides and you need to constantly repeat the habits and actions that cause it.

The Role of Habit Loop in Marketing

Understanding the habit loop has importance in the corporate world. All businesses require marketing and advertisement, and in a remarkable twist, most companies try to play on the habit loop to create a great, targeted marketing campaign. They try to slip in cues and remind you of the rewards of buying a new pair of shoes, for example. Given the fact that most companies also have a large enough database, they can streamline adverts directed to cause a desire within you.

This is even less subtle when it comes to social media. Many people have subconsciously formed an addiction to social media without realizing it. How does this habit occur? Well, most of the social media spaces, such as Facebook, Twitter, Instagram, and Snapchat, are designed to keep you hooked. They are built to tap into the habit loop and make it hard for you to resist them. Picking up your phone becomes a trigger that raises a strong desire in you to surf the internet. This act then generates a feel-good aspect that ensures that you are going to pick up the phone soon.

Identifying your habits

We cannot talk about changing your habits if you do not have a clear idea of what they are. You probably know the areas in your life that are causing discomfort, but you may not have closely considered why you're struggling in these areas. It's a good idea to reflect on things you may be doing (or not doing) that you should focus on. For instance, if you're trying to be healthier, are you drinking enough water? Are you eating as well as you suppose you are? Did you walk for 45 minutes, or only 30? If your saving account is something you're working on, how many times did you buy coffee instead of making it at home?

It took me years to finally identify the good habits and bad habits in my life, and the scary thing is that I didn't even think or put into consideration that I had any bad habits to begin with. Some of the habits that I identified was emotional eating (bored or stressed), social media addiction (morning and night), and irregular sleep. It wasn't until I started tracking my daily routine and how I go about my day, that I started realizing how some of these habits are harming my productivity, quality of sleep, and overall mood and energy.

Additionally with habit tracking, you can

Get Motivated

Having access to data that tells you just how much you have done can be a source of great motivation for you to stick it out. It doesn't even matter really if you have made big or small progress. Knowing there is progress of any form will make you more likely to stick to the process

Stay in better control

A tracker can help you know which habits you find hard to repeat and which ones are top of your list all the time. That will help you get to know your own desires better. Instead of randomly selecting some habits to change, you would have a veritable cache of hands-on data to support your choices.

Measure your progress

It becomes much easier to measure your progress in building a new habit or replacing an old one when you track your daily habits. That will help you decide whether you need to pick up the pace or let it slack. This is perhaps why most people try to track their habits.

How to track your habits

To track your habits, a good old-fashioned journal/diary can be pretty effective. You only need to fill in details of how many times you performed the habit every day. At the end of the week or month, you can look back at each specific day and form generalized conclusions. You can also use a spreadsheet if you prefer to use computers to keep track.

Aside from those more traditional methods though, your smartphone offers you a great choice too. We all go around with our smartphones these days, and a wide variety of habit tracking applications abound. Personally, I would recommend Momentum on IOS and Habit Bill on Android. I have used them in the past, and they were very effective in keeping me on track.

For every habit that you want to get rid of, you need to understand the key stages in its execution loop. You should be able to identify its trigger, the desire that causes it, the actual response (which is what you can see) and the psychological reward it offers you. The science behind breaking old habits uses this knowledge of the stages to defeat the habit. Knowing the trigger means you can try to reduce your contact with the trigger or minimize distractions. Understanding the desire and reward will help you design an alternative path for meeting the reward. You cannot defeat that habit until you have been able to identify its components and track it appropriately.

This is an example of a habit tracker that I often keep in my journal: I put a check mark if I completed the habit and I leave it blank or circle the box with a red marker on the days that I didn't! It's as simple as this.

 Daily Habits Tracker

	Mon.	Tues.	Wed.	Thurs.	Fri.	Sat.	Sun.
Habit #1							
Habit #2							
Habit #3							

Chapter Summary

Habits occur as part of a cycle of four events – the trigger, the desire, the response, and the reward. Each of these four stages must occur for a habit to occur. The effect of dopamine also helps to ensure that habits have a potentially increased chance of occurring. To change a habit, you must be able to identify it and the four components of its execution loop.

Reflection

1. What new habits do you want to start forming? List out 3-4 habits on the top of your head.
2. If you have started, are you tracking your habits? If you are not, you need to start. Track the number of times you complete that habit in a week through the daily habits tracker.

4

HOW TO MAKE HABITS WORK FOR YOU

"We first make our habits, and then our habits make us."
—*John Dryden*

How can you make your habits work for you? How can you optimize them to continue to produce results even when you are not putting in physical work? Achieving success shouldn't just be about setting goals and then burning all your fuel in a bid to attain those goals. Creating new habits shouldn't have to rely on blunt force and sheer willpower. Habits that you build that way are unlikely to last for long. Instead, the best way to make your habits work for you is by growing and fixing your mindset, prioritizing small steps, and finally, making a switch in how you see yourself.

Fix Your Mindset

Your mind is the most powerful tool that you can control consciously. Your mind, or more precisely, what you feed your mind will determine where you can get to in life. Success is a state of mind as much as it is a life goal. What our mind tells us constantly, we believe and work towards. Hence, if you keep telling your mind that you are not good enough to meet your targets, you will find it hard to complete those targets. Put simply, no one can go beyond where their mind takes them. That brings us to mindsets.

Your mindset represents the default state of your mind. It profiles your beliefs and creates a "standard operating procedure" for you. Basically, you will act according to what your mindset is. Therefore, if your mindset allows creative thinking skills to solve problems, you will find it easy enough to employ these skills to some degree of success. If, however, you do not even give yourself a chance to analyze the issues in front of you before bailing out, you will always lean to quitting as your first option.

Successful people have learned the importance of having the right mindset. That's why they are able to perform extraordinary feats. Thomas Edison, the famous inventor and businessman, was famed for his inability to quit. He was reported to have performed close to ten thousand experiments to perfect his invention of the light bulb. He was able to carry on for that long because his mindset dictated that behavior. Soccer player Cristiano Ronaldo is regularly known for his incredible mindset and competitiveness. The mindset he built for himself has made him one of the most recognizable athletes on the entire planet. Mention any successful person and you will find an unwavering, positive mindset behind them. That is why you must fix your mindset too.

Basically, there are two types of mindsets, the fixed mindset and the growth mindset. Individuals with a fixed mindset think of their abilities, chances, and aspirations in fixed terms that cannot easily be changed. So they define a comfort zone for themselves and stick around that zone for all their life. If circumstances threaten to take them out of this comfort zone, they are quick to resist and fall back within the threshold. Most people have this type of mindset.

The growth mindset, on the other hand, gives you a new perspective on your strengths, weaknesses, and targets. It lets you know that nothing is fixed or unattainable as long as you can work towards it. It lets you believe that you can be a better version of yourself by constantly seeking to improve your skills and knowledge.

Carol Dweck, a researcher at Stanford University, is well regarded for her work on the two types of mindset. She has charted the relative performance of people operating on the different mindsets and found this to say:

"In a fixed mindset, students believe their basic abilities, their intelligence, their talents, are just fixed traits. They have a certain amount, and that's that, and then their goal becomes to look smart all the time and never look dumb. In a growth mindset, students understand that their talents and abilities can be developed through effort, good teaching and persistence. They don't necessarily think everyone's the same or anyone can be Einstein, but they believe everyone can get smarter if they work at it," Dweck writes in *Mindset*.

The quote above is a perfect explanation for why many people cannot seem to make any progress or succeed. A fixed growth limits your horizon and forces you to think in closed terms. For instance, if you think a business idea is going to be hard to bring into fruition and you are not sure you can build a brand out of it, you have instantly damaged the odds of that idea becoming a success through you. If you say, "I am not good with relationships, then you have created a perfect excuse for not trying hard enough. You have given yourself exit options even before you make an entry. That means you are unlikely to try as hard as you should. Subconsciously, your mind will work to validate any setback as proof of the mindset you hold. In the same way, you will find it easier to foster the kind of habits that will promote your belief about your abilities. With each subsequent failure, you are less and less able to change your mindset.

It's obvious that a growth mindset is better placed to help us extract the maximum from our habits and beliefs. It plans for potential setbacks and leaves you willing to make another attempt even after failure. Since you believe you can improve, you have more faith in your abilities and prospects and will work with better focus and mental strength. You will be able to take criticism as a call for improvement and see failure as part of a learning curve.

Unfortunately, you cannot enjoy a growth mindset until you learn to rid your mind of negative assertions and beliefs. A fixed mindset will prevent you from making the necessary commitments to develop new, positive habits. Since you have created a ceiling for what you can do, you feel no pressure at all to change the *status quo*. To make a clean switch to a growth mindset, the first step is getting rid of all the negative beliefs you hold against yourself. You need to deal with thoughts and assertions like

1. Not everyone can succeed –I am just one of those who cannot.
2. I am not good with creative thinking.
3. I am not a born leader, and I find it easier to just follow other people's directions.
4. I will do the little I can. Maybe I am not built to do more.
5. I am average, and I need a lot of luck to succeed.
6. I am just lazy, and there is little I can do about that.

Negative beliefs like these render you incapable of substantial personal growth. In contrast, you can use positive affirmations to build up a growth mindset. Positive affirmations are short phrases or sentences loaded with positivity that you can repeat to yourself to build confidence. Examples of positive affirmations include

- I can do better than this.
- With dedication, I will achieve success.
- I have failed in this, but I am not a failure.
- I have limitless potential to grow and thrive in any situation.
- If anyone can do it, I can. If no one has done it, then, I will do it.
- My skills are not where I want them to be, but I will get them there in due course.

Positive affirmations can be repeated under your breath as you ascend in an elevator or while you wait for the bus. They can be written out and pasted in conspicuous areas such as above your mirror in the bathroom. The most important thing is to tap into them as a way of countering the effects of negative self-talk.

Take Small Steps

Do you know why it is so hard to sustain the new habits you develop? Often, we set huge targets or try to bluff our minds into accepting these habits. Feeding off the initial enthusiasm that got you to try out the new habit in the first place, it is easy to set lofty goals in the beginning. As the motivation drains off, though, it is harder to stay true to the habit and most of them just fizzle out on their own.

Let me use reading as an example. Have you ever tried to create a reading habit? How did you go about it? Most people would simply make a blanket decision to (1) try to read as much as possible (2) read a book every two weeks or (3) read 40 pages a night.

Here is the problem. The first option is simply too vague, and a lazy way of acknowledging that you need a change, but you are not willing to supply the commitment to make it happen.

The second decision can be overwhelming if you are not used to reading that much. It does not have any clear demarcations, and it is easy to miss the target with it. It sets too much work in front of you at once, and even if you try to sustain the habit for the first few weeks, you will soon lose the drive.

The third option does have a clearer plan to help you fulfill your intention. It is what most self-help books would advise you to do. The plan is obviously to shock your system into accepting that reading is a part of you now. The hope is that by reading a lot in successive days, you will come to accept it as routine. There is an essential flaw in this reasoning, though—it places too much pressure on you and you are literally working against the tide. It requires hard work and your mind may come to classify reading as a chore rather than a habit. Eventually you might hit a point where you decide to relax the rule, which leads you to stop reading. It may not be immediate, it may not even occur for a few months, but your mental resistance to the habit will win out in the end. It always does when the target is simply too high.

The surest, most effective way of creating a habit is to focus on consistency rather than the speed or volume of work done. Instead of following the usual channels that focus on the "big" goal at the end of the road, pay attention to the process itself and break down your journey into smaller chunks. Let us apply this to the reading example I cited.

What if you decide to read two pages every night? What does that do for you? Well, everybody can read two pages a night. It is so ridiculously small as a target that you cannot fail at it. That is the key! Since it is such a small target and is not in direct conflict with older habits, you do not even need willpower and motivation to pull it off. You just do it and forget about it till the next day. Gradually, though, your brain will start to understand that it is a vital part of your routine. A month or two down the road, and you will find that you have developed a reading habit without any extra effort. In fact, if the books you are reading are interesting enough, you will continue to read beyond two pages and be able to meet your goal every single time.

It is counterproductive to try to force the brain into doing anything it does not want to do. It will end in a lot of wasted effort and mental fatigue. Setting huge goals makes it harder for you to enjoy your progress. And to make matters worse, you cannot win with them.

If your goal is to lose twenty pounds by the end of the month, you will spend that entire month apprehensive and worried about missing your target. You may work incredibly hard at the gym to achieve your goal, but it's going to be hard for you to keep up with the needed energy to lose that much weight. The chances are high that you will get disillusioned and unable to cope with the stress after a short time. It is also possible that you will just get tired and quit along the way. Since you are making your brain work against its own inclinations, your entire body will be against the goal and it's harder to achieve it as a result.

Even if you do not quit, though, there is no way to win. Even if you miss your target by just two pounds, you will feel bad about not meeting it. Now, for all purposes, losing 18 pounds is just as good as losing 20 pounds but the only thing that will be in your mind is how you failed.

Now, let us imagine that you met your target. Hurray! You have lost twenty pounds. Now, what? Where do you go from there? Most people will simply spend the next month gradually filling up with the same foods they had banned and regaining the weight they have lost. In two to three months, you will probably be back where you started.

What's the way forward then?

When it comes to habit, consistency is key—not the amount of effort or time you dedicate to it. _In creating new habits, momentum is a greater weapon than willpower_. Our willpower is limited as humans; we simply have too many things to use it for. However, momentum can last for many years. By steadily building a habit in small, sure steps, you gently introduce it into your routine and allow your brain enough time to adjust. You do not need to disrupt your entire routine to incorporate a new habit. That will only set alarm bells ringing. Big goals are a big turn-off for the brain. Your brain isn't particularly interested in going through a whole month of punishing workout routines and starving yourself of the junk foods you are already used to, to experience the reward and joy that completing one goal brings. Yes, losing 20 pounds may be one big goal but it is still just one goal. When you break this goal into smaller, manageable chunks that are easy to complete, you are less likely to procrastinate. Best of all, you get rewards for every day you complete a small goal. It is really a win-win scenario for you.

The same thing applies to dealing with bad habits. Many people have failed to quit smoking by dropping their cigarettes one morning and declaring smoking banned. That takes more willpower than you have to enforce. The lure of a negative habit is always going to outweigh that quitting cold turkey. Instead, you should learn to chip away at your bad habits, block by block. Instead of having just one end goal, set up mini milestones throughout your journey and remember to celebrate or reward yourself for every milestone achieved.

Make a switch in identity

This is similar to a mindset change, only bigger. It's okay to learn to use small steps to build new habits and remove unproductive ones, but it is easier to create habits that are in line with who you think you are. What do I mean?

For instance, if you often stay up late to deal with your projects, you will find it easier to pick similar habits like drinking coffee in excess, rather than one like procrastination. Why? You have created a "night owl" persona and identity for yourself, and drinking coffee fits that identity.

Personal change, with respect to habit management, occurs in three distinct layers.

The first level at which change can be made is in your goals. This is what most people try to change. Building a successful business, finishing top of your class, losing weight, and becoming a great writer are all examples of changes in goals.

The second level is in your system. Many more people try to change the way they work towards their goals. This is where habit change features predominantly. You may choose to go to sleep early, read daily, visit the gym, and take a walk to reach new goals.

The third level, which is often neglected, is identity. This requires a complete overhaul of your working principles and beliefs. It is the most encompassing and thorough form of change and if successful, allows you to install a new catalog of habits.

I know it must sound daunting to you, but changing your identity isn't really as hard as it sounds. In fact, you need only two steps: (1) You need to decide who you are and who you want to be and (2) strengthen that identity by taking in consideration of what you should do and should not do as that identity.

Deciding who you want to be is the easier part. If your goal is to lose weight, for instance, then your identity is someone who eats healthy and enjoys going to the gym. Imagine yourself being that person, and start to re-evaluate all the actions you would or would not take.

Let me give you an example, you see a bag of chips in your kitchen pantry, taking in consideration the new identity you've start to associate yourself with, would you reach for that bag of chips and start mindlessly snacking on it? Or would you opt for something healthier in your kitchen such as bananas or nuts? Since your new identity is someone that eats healthy, you should obviously reach for the healthier food options, because it is who you are now! Learning to instill this type of thinking in your mind will help you tremendously throughout your habits transformation journey; you will then get to fix your system (the small habits that shapes your day to day), and finally get to reach to that big goal you've set for yourself (whether it is weight loss, job promotion, and etc.)

I will close this chapter with a quote from Frank Hall Crane. He said, "Habits are safer than rules; you don't have to watch them. And you don't have to keep them, either. They keep you." That is exactly why you must keep track of the habits you develop. They are the keys to your success.

Chapter Summary

To finally kick start that transformation you need, you must instill a powerful mindset in yourself. Having a clear identity and an idea of who you want to become will help you make the switch in mindset that is necessary for a complete overhaul of your habits. Then you can make permanent changes by investing in the power of small goals and habits, instead of focusing entirely on one single big goal or outcome.

Reflection

1. Choose a positive habit you would like to create for yourself. Why do you want this habit? Is it aligned with your identity?
2. Next, break it down into the smallest daily steps possible. Make the initial milestones as easy and simple as you can.

5

THE 5 GOLDEN AREAS TO YOUR LIFE

"You will never feel truly satisfied by work until you are satisfied by life"
— *Heather Schuck*

How important is work-life balance? I will illustrate with a story (told in her words) that a friend of mine, Christie, told me a few years ago.

"About five years ago, I had just opened a new bakery store. I had also decided to rebuild the online social media presence of the business and all that took me more effort than usual. My son was about two years old then, and he required lot of attention as children of that age do. I simply had more to do within the same amount of time. So I decided to stay up later than ever. I would put my son to bed, then spend an extra three to four hours working on new recipes, designing the website, replying to emails and reviewing one thousand ideas to solve the hundred problems I foresaw. I began to stay up later than ever and my whole body was adjusting to the fake adrenaline rush that my new-found caffeine addiction provided. I stayed up late and woke up even earlier than ever.

It was not uncommon to find me with bags under my bloodshot eyes on most mornings. I woke up grumpy and the spring in my step was almost gone. I was simply trudging through my days. Even my sex life was affected and I left my partner quite frustrated. That was not all, though. I lost some control over my emotions: I was more likely to snap at my employees when they made any minor mistakes, I experienced monumental changes. I worked harder than ever but enjoyed my successes less than ever.

This was simply because my emotional and physical health were off the usual wavelengths, even my career suffered and I was sure if went on longer, my financial health would have been affected. As for my relationships, they became strained and I was deriving less benefit than ever from them. Why? Simply because I had pushed my business to the fore and left everything else disorganized. Luckily for me, I realized what was happening soon enough. I started to delegate some of my tasks to trusted employees. That freed up more time which allowed me to give more attention to other aspects of my life. I restored my life balance and soon, even my productivity levels got boosted. If I had went down on the same path, living an unbalanced life, I know I would end up losing my business, family, and most importantly myself."

Many people suffer from the same fate as Christie. By neglecting one part of their lives for others, they distort the equilibrium they should enjoy and find it hard to get things done. What are these vital parts/aspects of life that must be taken care of? What must you do to ensure that you will get the right kind of balance? This chapter will deal with this and many more similar questions.

The components of life balance and wellness

What is Wellness?

Wellness means different things to different people, but what is the true definition of wellness? Being well involves achieving a healthy balance between wants and desires and achievements in different phases and areas of life. I consider the following five aspects of our lives as major components of wellness: financial, physical, emotional, professional, and your social health.

Financial Health deals with your personal finances and earning power. Earning a living is one of our primary duties as humans. Depending on the value different individuals bring to the table, we enjoy different levels of payouts and wages. However, the most important thing in financial health is being able to balance your wants and needs with your earning power.

Physical Health refers to general bodily health and care. You need to take proper care of your body. Adequate rest and sufficient exercise are a must at all times. It is also important that you keep yourself clean and seek medical advice whenever you are sick

Emotional Health deals with our emotions and how well we control them. Do you lose yourself to anger, panic, moodiness, insults, or jokes? Well, emotional health allows you to deal with stress and worry much more effectively. If you can become aware and develop your emotions in a way that they cannot affect your goals, life is much easier.

Professional/Career Health is probably the easiest to explain. We all want to rise to the top of our profession. We want to build a business empire that will leave us proud. The reality is that not everyone will create a multimillion-dollar business or rise to the top at their places of work. Luckily, everyone can improve or progress in their own ways and still feel accomplished like those who build big businesses.

Social Health has to do with forming healthy relationships with those around us. Social health can help maximize the psychological support you can receive from friends and family members. It is tied in closely with emotional health. Your disposition towards the social aspect of your life can have everlasting, long-term effects that you did not know. Everyone around you has better knowledge of something than you have. Learning to exist in harmony with them does wonders for your mood and gives you a lot of unexpected benefits.

None of the five aspects can be neglected if you aim to attain wellness and life balance. Even if you manage to supersede all expectations in four out of the five components but fail woefully in the management of the fifth, you cannot attain a state of wellness. The five components are interconnected. Poor performance in one of them will often lead to attendant consequences in the other. For instance, if you are stressed out by relationship issues (emotional), you may find it hard to eat and sleep adequately (physical health). This may lead to problems with productivity (professional health) and cause you some financial problems. All these can combine to damage your self-confidence and limit your interest in other people (social life). It is for this reason that you must pay attention to all aspects. These are crucial variables that will help you escape out of the LACK habit loop. That also means all your habits should work in balance with each other, to push you to improve each of the five key areas of wellness, just practicing good habits for a few areas of your life is simply not enough.

We will look at each of these aspects, one after the other. This next segment will focus on the area of financial health and will provide you with the habits right you need to achieve remarkable financial growth, starting today.

Small Habits to Big Changes

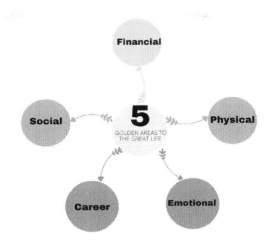

Chapter Summary

The five golden areas: financial, physical, emotional, career, and social health, determines the type of life we are going to build for ourselves, and how easy it is going to be to manage one's life. All five aspects work together in such a way that a loss of one affects all other aspects significantly and almost immediately.

Reflection

1. Can you identify which of the five golden aspects you have been neglecting? Why have you neglected it?
2. Can you list three ways you can improve on the neglected aspects? Is there any way to fix the neglect?

6

FROM SCARCITY TO ABUNDANCE: THE SECRETS NO ONE TOLD YOU ABOUT YOUR FINANCES

"If you look at what you have in your life, you'll always have more. If you look at what you don't have in life, you'll never have enough."
— ***Oprah Winfrey***

Understanding Financial Health

To be financially healthy, you must be in a state of mind where you have fewer worries about your income, wants, and expenditures. The term "financial health" itself is relative. You can earn exactly the same amount as the guy next door, seem to have the same sort of running bills to satisfy, and feel poorer than him. Why? Because he has a stronger & healthier financial mindset than you.

That is the difference between wealthy people and the rest of the world. If some quirk of nature or design happened to equally redistribute all the wealth in the world to everyone, I bet you that in short order, the majority of the wealthiest people right now will end up at the top once again in a few years. Why? They understand the principles guiding financial health, and they have mastered the art of staying financially comfortable. They operate at a different level entirely, while the vast majority of the world is stuck in one giant rat race, unable to break free to enjoy financial freedom.

How to Do More Than Just Break Even

Most people do not recognize that they live and earn just to break even. They do not know how to improve their financial well being, and they just scrounge along with the mindset that money is finite. In this section, I will focus on helping you do more than just break even and finally feel free from all your financial responsibilities. I will teach you how to improve your financial health by changing your mindset, setting the right financial milestones, and then implementing the best habits to bring you better financial returns.

The Scarcity Mindset vs the Abundance Mindset

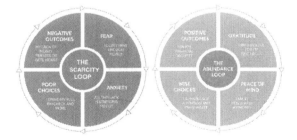

What do you think about money? What is your relationship with money like?

When it comes to your personal finances, do you think

- money is too hard to get
- you need to save hard to have more money

- you cannot quit your job because it's the only sure way to make money that you know
- the only way to make money is by working harder and taking on more shifts
- you cannot afford to chase your passions because they will affect the amount of money you have
- you are very unlucky in business, and just not cut out to make enough money

If you have these kinds of thoughts, then you have the scarcity mindset. You have made money into a scarce commodity that is hard to come by. You have decided that money is to be chased, not made, and somewhere at the back of your mind, you have also decided that you will likely not have enough money for most of your life. You have elevated money above your level of influence, and you are just happy to get the little trickle of cash that comes your way. You also think that the best way to increase the flow is to work harder at the job you have.

Theoretically, imagine that you work for $10/hour for five hours each day. One would expect that if you start to work for nine hours, you will make almost double your initial wage. In reality, though, it would take very little time for your expenses to catch up with your new wage and get you back to where you started from, with one notable exception – you will have even less time for yourself. You would only have succeeded in locking yourself even more firmly in a financial cage. The scarcity mindset transforms into a scarcity loop where you work harder to make more money, only to feel guilty for spending the money you have made. Because of the self-defeating beliefs you hold, it becomes an uphill task to make any substantial progress with your financial goals.

To make matters worse, the scarcity mindset makes you more susceptible to the **hedonic treadmill**. What is this? It's the concept that once your income increases, your wants and needs will change, and your overall spending will soar above previous levels. In the end, your disposable income will not increase even though the gross income has.

Contrast that with the abundance mindset that most financially independent people use. The abundance mindset believes that there is enough money at every point in time – you just need to create value that can bring you money. The time or the effort you put in is not directly proportional to your earning power, but the value you create is. The abundance mindset teaches you that there is enough money for everyone in the world, and the amount you can earn is dependent on the value you can offer. Since there is no limit to the amount of value you can learn to offer, that means there is no limit to the amount you can earn. People with the scarcity mindset see money as a master; those with the abundance mindset see money as a servant.

Money has no feelings, thoughts, resentments, or sentiments – it is very neutral. How much of it you are going to have is hugely dependent on what you believe about it. Therefore, when it comes to your chances of improving your financial standing, what you believe matters most. That's why two people with the same resources and will generate different turnover even if they are to go into the same business.

You cannot become financially independent until you learn to abandon the scarcity mindset. It imprisons you and puts your thoughts concerning money in a negative spin. The good thing is that you have a choice – you can choose to believe anything you want about money, and you will get to live according to those rules. Self-deprecating beliefs do you no good. They help you to stay rooted in scarcity; they set low ceilings for you and instruct you not to break through those ceilings. The scarcity mindset is most likely the root cause of all the bad financial habits you have built up over the years. In order to improve your life, you need to fix your habits, and in order to do that, first you need to change your mindset of who you think you are.

If you continue to think you cannot start your own business even when you have a novel idea that you have tried out successfully, it is likely that you will not start that business. Since you have failed to start the business, the amount of income you will generate will remain the same. Contrast this with another individual who is willing to take the required risks and go for gold. He takes the idea and runs with it. The margins of success he works with may be small, but they are much larger than the one you are working with. That's the difference between having scarcity and abundance mindsets. With the abundance mindset, you will become more of a doer, and improve your chances of success significantly.

One of the first steps in fixing your financial mindset is by setting up financial goals

Setting Up the Right Financial Goals

Too many people do not even have any sorts of financial objectives or goals. Others have unbalanced goals that do not really help them along the path to financial freedom at all. The right financial goals can liberate your thinking. For accountability's sake, you should establish the habit of having three clear types of financial milestones; short-, mid- and long-term.

Short-term financial goals are small targets that you can easily meet within a few days at most. They allow you to build up a lot of successive wins for motivation. Examples include taking time to check your finances, reading about the new business idea you have, and paying off a specific debt.

Mid-term financial goals take more time than short-term goals, and are also typically more challenging. They can include paying off the last part of your mortgage this year, or reducing your student loan debt by half.

Long-term financial goals are a representation of what you want to be in the distant future. Examples include saving up enough for early retirement, becoming completely debt-free, and building an online business. You are likely to run into more challenges with your long-term plans, and you should break these goals into smaller milestones, but it is also important for you to never lose sight of them.

What should you do with the three types of financial goals? Establish a habit – a routine in which you examine your short-term goals every few days, your mid-term goals monthly, and your long-term goals every six to eight months. This way, you will always know what your plans are, and when you make decisions on a daily basis, you will keep them in mind.

Good Financial Habits

If you are lost and unable to process what your financial goals should be, I present you with 5 proven habits that virtually everybody should aspire to achieve.

1. Be comfortable of saying NO

I have mentioned this earlier, but it's also very important to pay attention to this. Do not live above your means, and always feel like yes you need to buy the new iPhone, new bag, and new shoes. Be comfortable of saying NO to your wants and live below your means. It does not make any sense for your expenses to exceed your gross income. Don't confuse your wants with your need.

2. Budget for emergencies.

Life has a lot of twists and bends. Very few things ever go according to your plans when it comes to your finances. You will get unexpected windfalls like performance bonuses and an unexpected boom in sales, but you will also see unplanned emergencies like illness, a sharp decline in sales, or you may even lose your job. It can be hard to recover from such adverse events, especially if you have not planned for them. So you need to work towards creating a budget for emergencies in case things go wrong..

3. Remember to pay off debt.

Debt is one of the recurring staples of the scarcity mindset. It is easy to say debts can be good or bad, but the reality is that all debts take something away from you. The faster you pay them off, the better – because they take away part of your paycheck. They also make it hard for you to save and invest wisely. Worst of all, if you are bedeviled by a scarcity mindset, debts can become the cornerstone of your thoughts. So focus on paying off debts as quickly as possible. There is also the matter of compound interest; the longer you take to pay your debt, the more you will pay.

4. Investing.

You do not need a million dollars to start investing. An investment advisor is a valuable partner to have when it comes to managing your money, and will help your investment grow. Plan to invest for long-term returns, by the way. Unless you have lots of capital to begin with, you may need a bit of patience to see your portfolio grow.

5. Retirement Planning.

What is your plan for retirement? Do you intend to continue working at the same thing until you are deemed not fit to do what you spent your entire life working at? The entire goal of financial independence is for you to be free to pursue the things you want in life. Planning to retire early will help you create more time for your family and the passions you hold dearest. It's also very possible that your early retirement may get pushed back, but that is still much better than working until you're sixty-five. To this end, you need to start saving up and investing with an eye on early retirement. You want to save the bulk of your retirement budget early when you have fewer commitments, such as children to send to school. You do not want to start thinking about retirement when it's too late. Start now!

For every financial goal you set, you should work towards achieving it by building one or two habits that directly improve your chances of completing that goal. For instance, if you want to save up money to build a new house, you can choose to incorporate the habit of daily learning or reading about investing or ways to start a side hustle to increase your income stream. If you want to save more for retirement, you can take out an extra $10 per week for that. Setting goals is not enough; you must work towards them by building the right habits that enable you to get there.

Bad Financial Habits to Watch Out For

Your financial health can be compromised by bad habits. These habits will make it harder for you to attain your financial goals and can plunge you into years of debt.

Impulsive buying

Sometimes, we come across great bargains and we think that we need to make this unplanned purchase. That's all right, but if you seem to come across "*great bargains*" very frequently, something is not adding up. Impulse buying can ruin your budget and drain your savings. A shopaholic makes purchases because buying makes him or her feel good. Sometimes called emotional spending, being a shopaholic can upset your reward system can cause you to lose your financial bearings. You cannot tie your endorphins to making purchases. If you do, it will wreck your ability to meet financial goals.

Late Payments

Do not be caught trying to forget that you have debts to repay, the way a lot of people do. Well, unless you win a lottery (which is improbable), you will need to face your debts sooner or later. Wishing they went away doesn't get them any farther from you. Often, for credit cards you will incur a late fee & interest fees if you miss your monthly payments and fail to pay your balance in full. This is a terrible way to rack up more debt!

Keeping up with your friends.

No two people have the same purchasing or earning power, so trying to keep up with (or outdo) friends, family members, or colleagues when it comes to the things you buy is not a smart idea. It can cause you to live above your means and make unnecessary purchases. Keeping up is also guaranteed to create physical clutter in your home. When you have twice as many coats as you really need, you will need twice the space to keep your coats; you give over more of your home to your belongings.

Excessive Spending for Reward Points

There is a reason credit card companies offer you rewards for using their credit cards, and it's not because they want you to have more money. Rather, they want you to have more money *to spend*. An American study reported that making use of a rewards-based card with just a 1% return increases monthly expenditure by $68. That corroborates the fact that not all rewards-based cards should be used. If you can keep control of your urge to rack up those points, then it's fine to use them. If, however, chasing after points is your primary goal, you should get rid of them altogether. That will only end in one thing – more debt that needs to be paid off.

Living on Interest-free Loans

Interest-free loans can lull you into a false state of security. They are pretty much like credit card points in the way they cause to rack up loans you do not need. Things can get even worse if you have made a habit of not paying your loans until the grace period ends. The ensuing interest can put you underneath a pile of financial rubble.

Most people ruin their financial health with poor planning, expensive, unnecessary expenditures, a lack of clear financial goals, and a scarcity mindset that tells them to treat money with thinly veiled fear. You cannot afford to go down that route. You should look to set achievable and practical goals that can help you stay in better control of your finances. It's a key aspect of your life balance that you cannot just ignore.

Chapter Summary

Everyone is interested in boosting their earning potential and financial health, but are you doing the right things? Do you have the right habits? Boosting financial health has as much to do with increasing earning power as it has to do with securing a balance between your needs and wants. The right financial objective and habits, as always, will help you restore that balance.

Reflection

1. Identify all bad financial habits you currently have. How long have you had them for?
2. By a rough estimate, what percentage of your income goes towards needs and buying the things you actually require?
3. Think of 1 major financial goal you want to achieve in the next three months. Then draw up 2 habits to help you reach that target.

7
GET MOVING! GET PUMPING!

"Health is hearty, health is harmony, health is happiness."
— ***Amit Kalantri***

What is Physical Health?

Physical health goes beyond not being sick; being physically healthy involves making lifestyle decisions that keep you fit, avoid injuries, help you perform better at work, and stay in a balanced state of body and mind. Our health is a vital aspect and determinant of how well we can perform, everyone is aware of the importance of staying fit. We all know we perform better when our body is in great shape, free of fatigue and illness. Yet, somehow, people still mismanage their physical health.

In such a fast-paced world we live in today, everyone seems to be busier than ever. So we try to create more time by neglecting the vital components of our physical health. For that reason, we often see people not getting enough sleep or proper nutrition in the hope of putting in some extra hours of work.

Why You Should Look After Your Physical Health

It matters! Here is a newsflash for you – each time you compromise your physical health, your body becomes weaker and less capable of providing you with the requisite strength for you to succeed in the other key aspects of your life: work, relationships, emotional health, and relationships. Looking after your physical health will bring a lot of compound benefits to you. Bad health renders whatever progress you have achieved in other spheres inconsequential. How does physical health translate to a better quality of life?

Being physically active is one of the best things you can do to your body and your life. Physical activity gets every part of your body moving and active. A lack of physical activity is as big a factor in poor health as eating unhealthy food. By staying physically active, you can severely narrow the odds of diabetes, obesity, cardiovascular disease, and cancers. Physical activity also gives the immune system a boost, and it can also change your social life by boosting your self-esteem and helping you feel good about your body. When you are fit, you will be able to walk into any room with confidence.

In addition to physical activity, eating well has similar benefits to your body. It recharges your body and provides you with the right kind of nutrients in the right proportions, required to help you function optimally. Good nutrition habits will also help you sleep better, grow better and significantly reduce the number of sick days you take.

There is also a direct association between physical and mental health. Reduction in physical health immediately takes a toll on mental health as well. If you are not getting enough sleep or eating the right kinds of food, you would for sure end up feeling tired all the time and might even encounter sudden mood changes. In the same way, being depressed or anxious can cause you to pick up a bad habit that will affect your physical health, such as excessive alcohol use, lack of good sleep, and avoidance of exercise routines. It's a terrible cycle to be stuck in, and recognizing that is the first step in breaking out.

The Five Components of Physical Health

Physical health can be divided into five main components; sleep, physical activity, nutrition, hygiene and relaxation.

Adequate sleep

The human body requires sleep to maintain peak performance daily. Sleep is an oft-neglected part of our lives, but sleeping for fewer than eight hours a day is a recipe for distorting normal bodily functions. Physiologically, we have an internal clock, the circadian rhythm, that directs hormonal changes to produce a great sleeping experience. When poor sleeping habits cause you to fail to get enough rest, you are going against this mechanism and you are likely to make every new day a continuation of the previous day, instead of the fresh start it is supposed to be.

Physical activity

What do you visualize when you hear "regular exercise" and "physical activity?" For most people, these phrases evoke images of punishing routines at the local gyms or the aches they have come to connect with working out. Sadly, these images are false and can cause you to get too little physical activity. Physical activity starts from small details and choices such as ordering lunch versus walking around the corner to get it, and taking the stairs versus using the elevator. Choosing an exercise routine itself does not have to be the punishment you are dreading – there are countless options, and you can choose the most comfortable one for you. The only requirement is that you stay consistent.

Good nutrition

Your health is as good as what you eat. Eating healthily does not mean you must go on certain diet plans or fast. No! Eating well involves you sticking to ground rules – good habits that allow your diet to be filled with healthy food choices that can help you maintain proper weight, boost your immune system, and stay satiated. Good nutrition does not mean that you should restrict yourself from eating delicious food. It is all about nourishing your body with the right nutrients without going overboard. It's a matter of balance, like everything else in life. Sometimes you want to have ice cream for dessert, and that's totally fine, but most of the time you will try to eat more nutritious food that will fuel your body and mind with more energy.

Relaxation

You need some alone time to unwind and just relax your body and mind. Hobbies and sports are some of the best ways to achieve this. At times, you just need to forget about the intricacies of life, take a deep breath, and enjoy the breeze. Relaxation is a smart way of resting your body while enjoying every moment.

Good hygiene

Hygiene involves all the practices you choose in a bid to maintain your health and prevent diseases. Hygiene is basically concerned with staying as clean and neat as possible to reduce the contact you have with disease-causing microorganisms. This may include habits such as brushing regularly, wearing clean clothes, and keeping your fingernails neat. It also extends to cover preventive practices such as routine checkups to identify potential ailments as soon as possible.

Essential Good Habits

What are some good habits that you can adopt to help you stay in prime health? The best habits can be traced to the most important components of physical health.

- **Consistent bed time/wake up time!**

Adequate sleep is a must for you to enjoy the best physical health. While the body sleeps, brainwaves decrease in frequency. That means your brain gets to rest and recharge. The body's metabolic processes also decrease in intensity and you get the chance to catch up and perform some required repairs. It is important for you to get an average of eight hours of sleep every day for maximal health. It can be tempting to stay up late or steal some of the night to complete other tasks, but that is distinctly unhealthy. It is incredibly helpful to try to be consistent with what time you go to bed as well as the time you wake up, you are essentially training your body to adapt to the same habits so it will feel like your natural instinct. The more you do it the less you struggle with keeping it up!

Eating 3 meals/day

Another great habit is eating well, and try to aim for 3 meals/day. Good nutrition is the soul of good living. We require certain nutrients to live well, and your diet must contain all these essential nutrients. Fruits and green vegetables represent a source of many vitamins, minerals, and trace elements that can boost the immune system, facilitate proper metabolism, and allow you grow and develop as required. Having a consistent eating schedule will fuel your body with sufficient energy to help you stay productive and energetic all throughout the day. And no, that doesn't mean stuffing your body with pizza and diet coke, in fact that will probably exhaust your body due to slower digestions. You want to aim for food that is clean and easier to digest, the point here is not to make your body work harder, instead to provide all the energy it needs for your body to function at its 100%.

Exercise 15 mins/day

Regular exercise is also a must. It helps you stay fitter and healthier for longer. It boosts the immune system and gives you the required energy to complete all your tasks. The

Medical checkups at least 1x/year

Another important habit is regular medical checkups. Regardless of how well you look after yourself, illnesses are impossible to prevent totally. Therefore, you should take your checkups very seriously. The chances of surviving even serious illnesses like metabolic diseases and cancers increases when they are discovered in time. Closely tied to this is the need for hygiene. Primary good hygiene habits are a must-have. Regular baths, flossing, and dental checkups help you stay fresh and healthy.

Some Common Bad Habits that Damage Physical Health

When it comes to physical health, it's really an open-sesame situation. You get exactly what you put in. Olympic athletes are able to demonstrate such feats of endurance and strength because they stick to the right input. So if you eat well, get adequate exercise, and rest as appropriate, you will be better placed to enjoy better physical health than someone who spends their day binge-eating and nights watching Netflix.

Bad Nutritional Habits

What are some of the common nutritional habits that can severely affect your physical health?

Binge-eating

Overeating does you no favors. Rather, it will cause severe gastrointestinal discomfort, make you sluggish, and cause your body to excrete a lot of the consumed food, undigested. Binge-eating is part of the stress cycle, and is associated with increased debt, unproductivity, and procrastination. One potent trigger for binge-eating is the TV habit. Do you spend a lot of time on your couch, watching TV and munching away without a care in the world? Well, that habit alone can cause you to gain unneeded weight.

Consuming TOO MUCH processed food

Processed foods are foods that have undergone industrial processes before landing on the shelves of stores. Nobody has the right statistics, but the overwhelming majority of what people consume these days is processed food. The problem with processed foods is that they have not been produced to satisfy your nutritional requirements. Instead, profit is the main goal of the manufacturers. So they play to our sense of taste by making them sweet, spicy, and salty. Sugar addiction is a real threat to your physical health and processed foods are high in that. In addition, processed foods contain a lot of salts, preservatives, and additives that may turn out to be harmful to your health in the long run.

Smoking and excessive drinking

Smoking is responsible for one-third of all cancers (including 80% of lung cancers) and one-third of heart disease cases in the world. That people still smoke is really a tribute to the power that our habits hold over us. Alcoholism poses a similar health challenge. Some say that a glass of wine a day keeps the doctor away, but most people do not know that more than a glass of wine a day keeps the mortician in his job. Excess alcohol is poison for your body. The characteristic effect it produces is a fatty liver that can lead to death if not properly managed. Aside from that, alcohol can prompt you to gain more weight, leave you dehydrated, and produce unwanted social embarrassment when taken in excess. It also changes your brain chemistry and leaves you more vulnerable to stress and anxiety.

Bad Fitness Habits

As incredible as it sounds, you can still get things wrong with exercising and keeping fit if you have some negative habits. Some of these habits are discussed below.

Working out on an empty stomach

You need energy for your exercise routines, and food is the best way to fuel your workouts. You should eat about an hour before you hit the gym; it can make all the difference in the world. Working out on an empty stomach will mean you tire faster than you want and leave you feeling sore afterward.

Repeating the same routine

Your entire body needs exercise, so do not focus on only the areas you especially want to develop. You don't want a Dwayne Johnson type of upper body on legs that look like toothpicks. Aesthetically, that's a big no-no any day, and it's much less benefit to your body.

You need to challenge your body steadily. You cannot simply continue with the same routine forever. Over time, your body adapts to your usual routine, and the rate of improvement slows as a result. So you need to vary your routine frequently to continue to tap maximal benefits from your efforts.

Skipping your stretches

Virtually all professional athletes start and end their workout sessions with stretching – and it's for a good reason. Stretching out enables your muscles to get warm before more intense exercises start. That prevents the risk of muscle tears and injuries in general. It is the literal equivalent of getting used to the temperature in a swimming pool by dangling your legs in it (or taking a shower) before you dive in.

Lack of consistency

Slow and steady has been the message of this book, but you cannot exclude consistency from your routines. Even if your goal only calls for two sit-ups daily, ensure you complete them. There is a reason why you have set small goals in the first place. Do not allow inconsistency and procrastination to damage your plans.

How to Integrate the Right Habits for Your Health

To adopt and implement lasting positive habits for your health, you need to continue to take small baby steps that will lead to your destination. There is no hurry to pick up any habit; choosing one that isn't a good fit for you will only lead you to struggle and make it more likely that you will quit it. Rather than create an incompetent process, focus on two or three mid-term goals at once and allow small, consistent wins to build the way towards their permanence.

When it comes to your physical health, it is even more important to deal with negative habits fast. They can damage your health beyond repair, and priority should be given to such toxic habits like smoking, alcoholism, and overeating that can lead to metabolic diseases in no time at all. To do this, you will need to:

Identify these habits

Aside from the habits I have listed above, there are many other negative habits for your health. The good thing about these habits is that we can all tell when a habit is likely to affect our health negatively. The first thing to do, therefore, is to identify the negative habits you possess and mark them for elimination.

Cut off their triggers

Every habit has a trigger, as you know, and the most effective way of dealing with a negative habit is to prevent its trigger from being activated. You need to understand the trigger for the habit you are looking to remove and then work to ensure that the chances of it occurring are limited. For instance, if you often put off sleep to catch up on movies or tv shows, you may want to consider not bringing your laptop into your bedroom at all. That way, when you get into bed, you do not get distracted by the prospect of seeing a movie.

Develop alternative paths

Often, bad habits develop in response to a stimulus or need. Instead of fighting against the stimulus, you can provide an alternative, more productive path for the stimulus to get satisfied. For instance, when you get bored, instead of gnawing on your nails, you can simply stand up, do some stretches, and complete a quick workout routine. That should get your mind off your nails for the moment and keep your blood pumping.

Keep a Journal

We have talked about habit trackers and habit diaries in this book – and this is another application for them. Putting your routine or progress down on paper helps you gain some concrete feeling and control over what is going on.

All your goals and aspirations depend a lot on how fit and healthy you are. Physical health determines the limits to which you can go, and then it takes you there. For this reason, it is important to keep your body pumping and fit at all times. It will boost your productivity and confidence, keep you in good mental health, and allow you to build habits that can propel you to the upper strata of your potential.

Chapter Summary

We are only as strong as our bodies. Therefore, it is important to treat your body as the temple that it is. Physical health is required to make all the moves you need in other aspects of life. Good nutrition, proper hygiene, physical activity, and adequate rest combine to give you a sound basis for all-round development.

Reflection

1. Do you consider yourself a health-conscious individual?
2. How many hours of exercise are you getting weekly right now?
3. Plan out a daily target for your exercise routine. You could start small with as little as 15 minutes day, what's more important is consistency.

8
HOW EMOTIONS RULE YOUR LIFE

"Emotions influence every action we take. So the more we are aware of our feelings, the more we gain conscious control over our lives."
— *Jessica Moore*

Back in college, I shared an apartment with a roommate. We had enough parking space for our cars but on a cold morning, I had a good reason to be angry. My roommate's boyfriend had parked his car directly behind mine, making it impossible for me to get out. To make matters worse, they both weren't around that morning and I was running late for a final presentation for my psychology class. I kept calling her cellphone for almost thirty minutes before she picked up the call. I was understandably livid and I couldn't keep that emotion out of my voice. What made it even more frustrating was that she didn't even bother to apologize, she said "oh Jack and I just went for a morning run and didn't realize you were going to class already. We're running back now, be there in a few." They came back fifteen minutes later...

I was extremely annoyed and I muttered angrily under my breath as I drove to class. I was worked up and sweating as I arrived fifteen minutes late to my presentation. I didn't greet anyone as I made my way into class and I screwed up my face in a frown each time someone came up to me that day. I ended up doing ok on the presentation, but I knew I could have done ten times better if I had been in control of my emotions. Throughout that day, I was off balance and it showed in every aspect of my day. When it was time to write in my journal that night, I reviewed my day and realized that my anger had got the better of me, and I had run the entire day on an emotional rollercoaster.

Just as we are creatures of habit, we are also creatures of emotion. Our history, current circumstances, and prospects for the future all contribute to determine the kind of emotions we experience at every point in time. At every moment, we are the subject of emotional impulses that seek to direct our thoughts, beliefs, and actions. They are basically reactions to certain occurrences or our state of mind, and should not form the bedrock of our actions and reactions.

Emotions can be positive, such as joy and excitement, and inspire positive thoughts that can lead to great outcomes. Or they can be negative, such as anger, grief, sadness, or confusion, and threaten to tear apart the health we currently enjoy.

Therefore, emotional health refers to your ability to stay in control of your emotions, even when they are at a boiling point. Emotionally healthy people realize that they need to stay in control and not go on reactive actions due to their emotions. They learn and showcase the art of bouncing back even in the toughest of times. Because they can manage their feelings, they can stick to their goals and processes in times of major upheaval. Being in great emotional health also directly helps you stay in better physical and mental health. Therefore, it is necessary to be able to rule your emotions and not allow them to rule you. This chapter will show you how.

Why do you need to be emotionally healthy?

Great emotional health does not mean you are happy all the time. Rather, the goal is to be able to process your emotions, turn off the mental heat they generate, sort them out, and then act accordingly while in full control of yourself. Being able to do these things will certainly give you certain advantages.

With good emotional health, you will become more resilient in the face of adversity. You will come to understand that even the most negative emotions do not last forever. That may be the glue that holds you together when you are grieving or deeply sad. Good emotional health will not mean you deny the existence of pain or any other negative emotion. Instead, it will teach you to take them in stride. You will become resilient, and negative emotions will be unable to change your psychology for long.

We are all going to suffer setbacks and face obstacles in our desire to succeed. Some will be as a result of our choices and actions; others will come from external factors. There is no way to attain success without coming across these setbacks, but by keeping your emotional health in good shape, you can learn to weather all storms and remain firm in your decisions and plans.

In addition, good emotional health will help you develop deeper and more meaningful relationships. As someone in charge of their emotions, you will enjoy feelings of love and companionship better than ever, and be wise enough to realize that negative emotions are part of the overall package as well. Sometimes, chronic negative emotions can lead to further complications such as codependency and low self-esteem. In particular, low self-esteem is often the product of uncontrolled thoughts and negative emotions that make you feel inadequate or not good enough for the things you want. When emotional health is poor, you may suffer from depression and anxiety, which are triggers for developing an unhealthy level of self-confidence and self-esteem.

The same thing applies to anger and panic. Anger can be overwhelming if you allow it to control you. One of the primary reasons you should work on your emotional health is to be able to exert control over blinding, negative emotions such as low self-esteem, pain, anger, panic, and grief.

Aside from helping you deal with negative emotions, good emotional health often has similar effects on your physical health. Every surge in emotion, positive or negative, produces corresponding physical reactions. When we laugh, we feel light-hearted, relaxed, and free. When we receive bad news, our entire body feels heavy and slow. We may be prone to headaches or upset stomachs. Poor emotional health can also leave you susceptible to illnesses by reducing the sentinel action of the immune system significantly.

Cutting Out the Pitfalls

There are several ways by which you may damage your emotional health without even realizing it. Some people have very poor emotional health due to the way they were brought up and their experiences in childhood. Other people have allowed bad habits to chip away at their emotional health for too long. Whatever the case, knowing the type of bad habits that can destroy emotional health is the first step in getting rid of them.

Being in a relationship with a narcissist can be draining, and a tough ask for anyone. A typical narcissist prides themself on being able to manipulate their partner to do their bidding, and can go any length to satisfy these selfish desires. Partners of narcissists often suffer from issues such as low self-esteem, inability to process emotions, and a fear of confrontation. All these can lead to an unhealthy emotional balance. Now, you may be confused about how having a narcissistic partner can be a negative habit. Well, most victims of narcissism become codependent – they come to rely on the abusive partner to an unhealthy degree. They make a habit of trying to please their narcissistic partners.

Even if your partner is normal, if your relationship is an unhappy one, you need to consider its effect on your emotional health. Living with the frequent disagreements, unmet needs, and frustration of an unsuccessful relationship is stressful and takes a toll on your emotions.

Emotional balance is not the only thing that a toxic relationship can destroy, though. It can destroy your confidence through excessive criticism, and make you question yourself. Is there a little voice in your head that whispers all your doubts and fears? Do you often catch yourself saying or thinking things about yourself that are not so nice? It is good to do an honest self-assessment once in a while, as long as it is constructive. This can help you to realize mistakes early enough to correct them and keep you grounded in facts. However, having a fountain of destructive criticism within your own thinking is a recipe for emotional disaster. If you cannot find yourself worthy, you will find it hard to deal with negative attention that may come from other people. That little voice in your head can destroy your emotional health faster than any other thing. If you leave it switched on for days on end, you will come to believe what it is telling you, and that will cause emotional chaos for you.

Your physical health can also affect your emotional health. As an extreme example, someone who has been bedridden for a long time may be overwhelmed by negative emotions arising from his condition. Again, being obese or unfit can cause problems with self-esteem and cause you to lose confidence. This can also snowball into more fundamental emotional problems such as comparing yourself negatively against other people.

You need to stop comparing yourself, your abilities, and achievements in a negative light with other people. We aren't built the same way, and we don't function alike. So the habit of constantly comparing yourself to other people is self-defeating. The practice trains you to look for signs that confirm your working hypothesis that you are not good enough. This can make you feel depressed, angry, or bitter about your own personal achievements.

The RIGHT Habits to Foster your Emotional Wellbeing

To achieve emotional balance, you should consider adopting some of the habits below.

Learn to express your feelings

Bottled-up emotions do not go away on their own. They simply lurk around in your mind and cause a lot of confusion for you. It is necessary for you to be able to express your emotions all the time. If someone has offended you, speak to them or find a way to forgive them. Do not just allow seething rage to destroy your emotional balance.

Manage stress

Stress is one of the most harmful causes of emotional imbalance. Prolonged exposure to stress hormones like cortisol and adrenaline is very hard on your body and has been linked to health issues such as high blood pressure, ulcers, and even cancer. When we task our body beyond its limits regularly, the ill effects can be long-lasting. Try to resolve, or at least reduce, the stress you go through on a daily basis: do not spend time with people who make you feel drained or irritated; do not read the news if it's affecting you; take a break; get some exercise. A stressed-out individual is going to find it extremely hard to stay in control of their emotions because their mind is always boggled with the next problem.

Get adequate rest

Adequate rest and sleep can do wonders for your mood. Sleeping for at least eight hours will help you recharge your emotional batteries and wake up feeling refreshed and ready for the day's activities.

Try to stay positive and practice gratitude

Optimism is a key staple of positive emotions, and pessimists always seem to find ways for destructive self-criticism to thrive and flourish. If you want to reap the benefits of sound emotional health, invest in an optimistic outlook. One thing that helps with this is making it a habit to write in a gratitude journal, especially if you can do this in the morning. This practice teaches you to focus on things that are making you happy and relaxed, and it's surprising just how much it can shift your mindset from negative thinking to positive.

Learn to seek and access help

No man is an island; from time to time, we all need support from our family members and friends. Do not deny yourself these vital allies in your bid to access better emotional health.

It isn't always easy to share personal details, but over time it becomes easier and it's a healthier and more natural way to live.

You should also make a habit of seeking formal therapy for more serious mental health conditions like anxiety disorders, post-traumatic stress disorder, and depression. These disorders will make it almost impossible for you to enjoy good emotional balance, so seeking treatment for them is the first step in your recovery phase.

Practice Meditation

Meditation has many mind-relaxing benefits, but if you find yourself on the wrong side of the emotional health scale, it is even more important than ever to start a meditation routine. Meditation will allow you to get into a relaxed frame of mind where you can come to acknowledge your emotions and thoughts without allowing them to weigh you down. By practicing a consistent meditation routine, you can melt stress and anxiety away and get to the core of who you are. Meditation allows you to enjoy what proper emotional health should look like. It is a non-negotiable habit that you must establish.

To conclude this chapter, let me reiterate that nobody is immune to negative emotions. We all react to things in much the same way, but emotionally healthy people are smarter in dealing with their emotions – they embrace them and do not run away from them, and they learn to stay on an even keel. That alone is enough reason for you to work on developing your emotional balance and stability.

Chapter Summary

Emotions are powerful – they are always present and in charge of our actions. Until you can deal capably with your emotions, there will be an internal conflict that can reduce your ability to succeed in the other important aspects of your life. Stress and toxic relationships are the two most major threats to emotional security. Therefore, you must focus on having the right kind of relationships and staying ahead of stress.

Reflection

1. How well do you manage your emotions? On a scale of one to ten, how likely are you to get angry on a normal day?
2. On a scale of one to ten, rank how stressed you are at the at the end of the day for the next two weeks. What was your average score?
3. Which of the good emotional habits do you plan on implementing in your life to improve your emotional health?

9

GIVE YOUR CAREER A BOOST

"The worst days of those who enjoy what they do are better than the best days of those who don't."
— *James Rohn*

Do you like what you do? Does going to work fill you with excitement and genuine enthusiasm? Are you in that job because you love it, or just because it pays the bills?

These are important questions that we often ignore, but your answers to these questions can help you execute the greatest evolution of your life. Far too many people do not enjoy their careers, and the negative effects of this spills over into all aspects of their lives. A career goes beyond just paid work, though. A complete definition for "career" would encompass all the things you do daily in pursuit of satisfaction. It could be work, running a business, schoolwork, or even volunteer work. The best way to put it would be that your career represents an overview of all the layers of your personality that deal with accomplishment, including training, education, volunteerism and research throughout your lifetime.

We are always in one career or another. From the very first class you attended as a toddler, you learned to invest effort and time in the pursuit of career and related goals. You may be in that career because you want to make money, but at the same time, as much as your career represents your main mission in life, you have to strive to create a balance between your career and other important aspects of your life. You cannot neglect your family or health, for instance, to focus solely on your career. The imbalance that would cause is bound to generate negative ripples in every aspect of your life.

This chapter will teach you why you need to maintain a healthy career balance, develop the best habits to grow your career, and enjoy the best the world has to offer. The golden rules of career growth say you must

- **like** what you do
- **great** at what you do
- **get compensated** for what you do

Your career goals must feed into your vision of who you want to be. Your career should be something you want to succeed at. If it isn't, you won't have a natural flair for it or the resilience required to grow. At the same time, you must try to continually improve and attain your target goals. These may be things like a promotion, starting your own business, or getting a Ph.D.; whatever it is, you need to want it bad enough and then develop habits that can help you achieve it. There is a caveat though – you need to enjoy what you are doing to enjoy career health. Let me explain further.

If Paul is good at what he does but does not love it, does he feel like a success? No! The time he needs to spend on his work is not enjoyable to him, and so it feels like a lot more effort to achieve success. That will take a toll on other aspects of his life. That also means he doesn't really have a great career. Contrast this with Michelle, who is not the best at what she does currently, but she likes it and works at it with a strong passion to improve her skills. Such a person would have no limit to how far she can go. She would be able to commit herself to steady improvements and stay the course for longer because she enjoys her role. It's not about how good you are at something now, it's about how much dedication and hardwork you are willing to put in to make yourself the best! It is that simple, it breaks my heart when I think about how many people spend twenty or thirty years into their so-called "career" and knows deeply in their heart that they hate their job, yet fail to take the proper leap to pursue something else that aligns more with their interests…I can teach you all the effective habits you need to know to boost your career health, but the real question you need to ask yourself too is: *"Are you in the right career?"*

Happy Career, Happy Life!

How important is it to have great career health? I am sure this is one of the easiest questions you could have to answer. Besides the more obvious reasons, here are a few more why you need to work to continue to improve to the next level of career development so that you fulfill the three golden rules of a successful career.

Your relationship with your career can be a huge factor in how much stress you face. If you are constantly overworked, underpaid, or unmotivated, it's more likely you will become overwhelmed by both physical and mental factors. Working under highly-strung or fast-paced conditions can leave you stressed out and unable to maintain proper balance.

On the other hand, a positive working environment can transform your temperament for the better. People with great careers and consistent improvements often find their happiness spilling into other aspects of their lives. Life is easier when you get to work with a smile and leave work with a smile. When that happens, it's likely that you will have that same happy disposition everywhere.

Unfortunately, the reverse is also true. Work pressure can easily seep into your life and distort many other things. For example, suppose Jerry comes home late after a particularly stressful day with board meetings that centered on his team not performing well enough. He is now under pressure from the CEO to cut at least four people from the team. However, he knows his team did better than the results showed and he is at a loss as to who to cut from the team. He comes back home to meet the kids playing in the living room, and just as he steps in, his eldest son throws a toy car, which smacks Jerry on the head. Instantly, he transfers his aggression and roars at the kids. The youngest one begins to cry and his wife comes rushing to see what happened. A big fight ensues, all due to the built up tension from work.

Of course, positive and negative events in your career can take a direct toll on your relationships. I will discuss more about this in the next chapter, but there is no real way to isolate your career from your relationships. A great relationship can provide you with maximum support for your career and afford you better resilience. On the other hand, toxic relationships can spill into your career and make it harder for you to enjoy career satisfaction.

Apart from your relationships, the lifestyle habits you adopt to further your profession can take a toll on your health if not properly chosen. For instance, if you use a computer constantly, you should look to get protection for your eyes. Also, sitting for long periods and a bad sitting posture can cause discomfort and injury. Your career also determines the kind of financial security you are going to enjoy. Passion or not, we all want to live well enough, and our careers often represent our plan for financial security. That is one reason we go into them in the first place. Usually, improved career health translates to improved financial health. So if your career health is great, you have a better chance of being able to meet your financial goals. That alone can save you some emotional grief in the long run.

Bad Habits that can Affect your Career Health

It's not rocket science to say that your career is where it is because of the decisions and habits you have made its cornerstone. Smart, successful people make use of smart habits that can give them the professional boost they want. On the other hand, certain bad habits can disrupt your work-life balance and make it impossible for you to enjoy career health.

Lack of learning and growth

Another bad habit is staying stagnant or not being aware of new trends. Are you improving your skills or just going along with the flow? It's possible to get so comfortable that you forget to learn new trends and apply them to your career. Constant learning is a foolproof way to stay at the top of whatever game you are playing. Do not get lulled into doing the same things every day for a whole decade. Always switch things up, learn new ways of doing your work, and be ready to take risks on new methods.

It is never too late to perform a career switch. It's quite easy to land in the wrong job for you, but it is unforgivable to remain in that profession for too long, knowing that it is indeed wrong for you. Fear is often the primary reason people find it hard to make a career shift. You may be besieged by doubts about the future, but if you fail to live in the present by your own rules, the future might just be as drab as now. Sometimes you do not even need to change your entire profession to find what you enjoy doing. You can switch things around, change the way you do things, and vary your overall outlook. You just might find the best career choices that way. Remember, even in an unsatisfying job, you have picked up many useful skills.

Being too rigid with your untested or outdated principles can also ruin your progress. You need firm principles, but you also need to adapt to current realities. *Blackberry* and *Nokia* are two famous examples of companies that lost a large percentage of their formidable market share because they failed to adapt to current demands and changes in what consumers wanted. They stuck to the same ideas and habits that had served them so well in the past. Today, they are not where they used to be. In the same vein, you must not become so committed to principles and plans that you become blind to the signs in front of you. If your work is threatening your relationships, for instance, maybe you can consider closing an hour early to provide and receive some needed companionship. If your hiring policy has consistently delivered below-par employees, you should look to reflect on how to fix it, instead of holding on to a system that doesn't work. Create habits and a working style that are reactive to change around you and open for improvement.

Perfectionism

Going after perfection is another bad habit. On the surface, being a perfectionist looks like a great way to maintain motivation and generate momentum while ensuring your standards are never dropped, but perfectionism actually hurts you before long. With perfectionism, you are driving through life at maximum speed with a turbo boost. Sooner or later, that boost is going to end and leave you unable to adjust to realities. Perfectionism can make you place unattainable targets that will take more mental energy than you have left in your tank. It can also make you prioritize wrongly, take on more work than you can handle, and affect other areas of your life.

Not being a team player

One such bad habit is being unable to work as a team player. As different individuals, we have different personalities. Some people work better alone; they revel in the freedom that gives them to make all the decisions and even complete all tasks on their own, but that is hardly ideal in the long run. "Two heads are better than one" is very often proven to be true in the workplace. Delegation of tasks to other people can help you free up time to focus more on the control and management side of the business. Working as a team player means you are able to see issues from different points of view, and there's a greater chance that you will cover all the necessary bases. Unless your business or work is on a very small scale, being able to work with others will provide you with a great boost.

Good Habits for Achieving a Solid Balance

When it comes to the ultimate career success stories, there is no better place to look to than people who have done it – the Jeff Bezoses, Richard Bransons, and Mark Cubans of the world. These men have all cultivated top habits that have allowed them to leap the usual hurdles and maximize their career health. Let's take a look at how you can attempt to create a similar balance.

Plan your day

Almost all motivational authors and performance strategists agree that having a clear plan for the day helps you do more. A clear plan, in more ways than one, can ensure your daily tasks align with your targets and goals. Instead of trying to just take everything in your stride, a clear plan means that you know exactly what you have planned for each day. You know what you will be doing at every point of the day and why you are doing it. In planning your day, though, you need to know your peak intelligence time and plan to do the heaviest part of your work within it.

For instance, I have found that I am most productive between 5:00 a.m. and 9:00 a.m., so I wake up early and get going with my routine. I allow my peak intelligence time to coincide with an active period. This may differ for you, but you have a peak intelligence period too – everyone does. Some have found that they perform best early in the morning, others rightly believe they are night owls who work better at night. If you can schedule most of your tasks and challenges to be resolved within this time, you have a boost. The nine-to-five routine may not suit you, so if you are in a position to be flexible with when you work, ensure you work more around your peak intelligence time. It makes all the difference

Be proactive

What do you spend the majority of your day doing? Are your tasks more focused on what you are doing, or what other people are doing? This is an easy pit to fall into. If your day consists mainly of tasks that involve you trying to catch the attention of other people, respond to their inquiries, and generally react to messages and ideas, you may not be enjoying the best of your creativity. The easiest example of being active is in the way we reply to emails. If you spend the best part of the days responding to emails, you have put yourself in a reactive mode, where your creativity is stifled. Emails also take more time than you realize. For this reason, manage the way you respond to them and the amount of time they take from your daily schedule. Stay active; try to get in more work that is focused on breaking new ground rather than reacting to existing communications that could wait until all the proactive tasks are complete.

Closely allied to this is active brainstorming sessions – you need to have more of them. Asking the right questions is a good way of forging ahead in your career, but have you been doing enough of that? You need to constantly look at ways to solve existing challenges and potential problems. Brainstorming can be in a group with colleagues, or you can do it mentally. If you do not think, you cannot discover new ways and advance new methods. Brainstorming allows you to ask the right questions

Limit meetings

Meetings seem great – they give the whole team quality time to discuss and agree on approaches and tasks to be done. Right? Well, meetings can also be a huge problem when it comes to time management. The truth is, most meetings simply take too much time – the decisions or advantages they offer are often inferior to the amount of time and collective effort they take. The ideal thing, if it is within your power, is to limit the number of meetings you attend. Chuck some of them in the bin if you can, and use the time you have saved to work on more productive ends. You will not be able to escape all meetings but at the very least, try to reduce the average time each meeting takes from you. This is even more practical if you are the boss or employer.

As Mark Cuban, owner of the Dallas Mavericks said, "Meetings are a waste of time unless you are closing a deal. There are so many ways to communicate in real time or asynchronously that any meeting you actually sit for should have a duration and set outcome before you agree to go."

Start the day with small wins followed by a big bang

This is a personal habit that I employ daily. Building up some small wins early in the day gives me confidence for the rest of the day to complete the harder projects, so I have built a routine that includes habits that support my mindset. My early morning wins include meditation, exercising, reading, and writing in my gratitude journal. Then I get to work on my biggest tasks right away. By the time I get started on my biggest tasks, I am already imbued with confidence and motivation to work efficiently.

Distraction-free zone

The internet is a great thing – you can learn and be entertained by its various offerings. However, getting addicted to the internet is a potential career drawback. It's the most common distraction available to us these days. If you get sucked up into the net or social media when you should be working, it reduces your productivity drastically. You'd be amazed by how much of your day is being eaten up! To boost productivity, you need to be able to manage the amount of time you give to the internet, especially on fruitless endeavors. A number of productivity apps can even help you with defeating that habit – an example is *StayFocused*. The tool alerts you after a window period and then proceeds to actually block the offending sites. Other similar trackers can help you track just how much time you spend on the net. If you are having serious productivity issues because your phone is a big distraction, then it's time to get it away from you. Put it in a bag or drawer when you have work to do, or leave it in a different room entirely. Your phone can be the BIGGEST distraction for you and if you want a truly successful career, you cannot spend three hours on social media scrolling through other people's lives. You have to live your own life –

and that starts with getting rid of your phone when you have work to do.

Chapter Summary

Your career takes up the largest part of your day. It is what you want to make out of life, and represents perhaps the largest share of where your efforts go. Therefore, you cannot afford to be in the wrong career. At the same time, your career should not overwhelm you so much that you lose sight of every other thing. You need to aim for that perfect balance between work and life.

Reflection

1. On average, how many hours do you spend working in a day? Do you feel like the your time at work goes by slowly or at a quick/decent paste?
2. What sort of environment do you work in? What's the overall mood at work like? Do you enjoy this type of environment/mood?
3. Do you feel dreadful going to work everyday or do you truly enjoy it?

10

LEARNING TO CONNECT

"When nobody around you seems to measure up, it's time to check your yardstick."
Bill Lemley

As children, we ran into the comforting arms of family members when we felt threatened by anything. When we felt happy: we also ran to our family but with laughter, joy, and love. We learned to trust in their affection for us and use that connection with them as the bedrock of our aspirations. What if I tell you that you might be an adult now, but the role of your relationships hasn't changed? Yes, we still have relationships to fall back on and draw support from. Unfortunately, many people seem to have forgotten this. This chapter will deal with the impact of social health on our entire wellbeing.

What is social health?

We are the dominant species on planet Earth – not because we are the strongest or fastest, but because we have learned to work together, and this is the reason we are wired for relationships. In fact, the entire human race is just one network of relationships between people, families, and society. No single man is an island unto himself, and few can claim to be truly independent. Given the important role that relationships hold in life, it is no surprise that people who build very strong, healthy, and mutually beneficial relationships enjoy the best that life has to offer. This chapter is going to be about your social health – the way you interact with the people you meet, and how you can tap into the benefits that healthy relationships offer.

I like to use Atul Gawande's description of what social health is. It says, "Human beings are social creatures. We are social not just in the trivial sense that we like company, and not just in the obvious sense that we each depend on others. We are social in a more elemental way: simply to exist as a normal human being requires interaction with other people."

Staying socially healthy requires you to build positive relationships that can offer you a strong support system as you chase your goals. The right kinds of relationships can lift you to meet your potential and make it easier for you to do what you need to do to thrive. We are in some relationships that we didn't get to choose (or didn't realize we could choose) – you don't get to choose your parents, siblings, children, and most family members. Sometimes we do choose – you get to select who you want to be friends and partners with.

More importantly and less noticed, though, is choosing the kind of relationship you want to have with everyone you come in contact with. Social health also includes knowing which relationships to manage carefully, which ones to terminate, and the right reasons for terminating such kind of relationships.

When social health falls below appreciable levels it causes loneliness. Often, a lonely person fails to acknowledge the relationships around them that can help them and continues to live in emotional and mental isolation even though this is painful. Loneliness can be caused by a number of factors, but it's important to address the problem. Companionship is the natural order of things. It gives your social health a boost, and you will learn to enjoy the notable perks that the people around you bring to the table.

Your social health has a lot to do with the way you are brought up and the kind of person you are. Luckily, it doesn't matter if you are an introvert or extrovert; everyone has the same chance to spruce up their relationships and make them better than they currently are.

The Importance of Social Health

Why do you need strong social connections? Why should you get out of your little cocoon and extend the hand of friendship to your neighbors? Well, social health comes with a lot of positive benefits for you and your long-term goals. When it comes to productivity, strong relationships at work can improve your efficiency.

"The workplace is not a place to socialize" is one of the greatest fallacies of this millennium. It's true that romantic relationships can *sometimes* get in the way of overall business goals, but thinking you should not or cannot have meaningful relationships with the people you share an office with every day is a big bag of illogical thinking. On the contrary, developing healthy ties can help you work better. To prove this, Margie Warrell, a Forbes contributor, rehashed the result of a Harvard Business Review study. She explained that the findings of the study suggest that team performance can be increased by half if members connect on a social level. Clearly, good social health has a positive impact on our professional health.

Social health also impacts positively on physical health. How? A study at the University of Minnesota discovered from a literature review that encompassed 148 different studies that people with healthy interdependent relationships are 50% less likely to die prematurely when compared with those in toxic relationships. This is another important reason to take a close look at relationships that are difficult for you, and consider setting firmer boundaries or even ending those that are taxing your mental and emotional health. It doesn't seem like it's a life or death, but if left to fester, it can be.

In addition, loneliness has been reported to be a primary depressant of the immune system and can leave you susceptible to things like heart disease, stroke, and cancers.

Steve Cole, an associate professor of medicine at the David Geffen School of Medicine, had this to say about loneliness: "(Our study) showed that the biological impact of social isolation reaches down into some of our most basic internal processes – the activity of our genes. We found that changes in immune cell gene expression were specifically linked to the subjective experience of social distance." This was not the first time a study had made the same claim. A 2011 study had predicted the same thing. People who do not enjoy healthy relationships have weakened immune systems, and fall sick more often.

Many other scientists have put forth statements that loneliness and a lack of human connection is very unhealthy, some even going so far as to suggest that it's as bad as smoking. You get the picture: loneliness kills.

Deeper relationships can also bring you other emotional rewards. How? They provide great support for you. The easiest way to switch from a sad mood to a better mood is by calling a friend – we all benefit from spending time with people we care about, people who care about us. Even your personal achievements feel better with the people you love around you. The desire to please our loved ones encourages us to try even harder. In return, the people we form strong bonds with can be the listeners we need when we are confused. Family members can be a source of emotional support during trying times. Knowing people care about you is a great motivation to do the best you can in everything.

Bad Habits that Inhibit your Social Health

It is easy to blame everyone else for your loneliness, but the fact remains that you have contributed more to your social wellbeing (or lack thereof) than anybody else. That means your habits have played a primary role in deciding how strong your relationships with other people are, the dynamics of the relationships, and the level and amount of benefits available for you to enjoy from your relationships. Some habits promote loneliness and make you less likely to reach out to create friendship bonds, or acknowledge honest overtures of friendships.

The most common excuse and reason for a disturbed work and life balance is "I am too busy." Being too much of a workaholic leaves you with too many bridges to cross in your relationships. "All work and no play made Jack a dull boy." Work is important – we talked about that in the last chapter – but you need to create some time for the people around you. Total immersion in your work can make it harder for you to appreciate those around you.

You also need to be willing to offer as much emotional support as possible to those people around you. You need to be able to see their vision and offer them encouragement. Don't just reach out when you need something.

Despite your hopes and wishes, do not expect all your relationships to be awesome or mind-blowing. It's unrealistic to think that every romantic partner is going to make you feel like Romeo or Juliet; not every new friend is going to pull out all the stops for you. So don't create unrealistic daydreams about what your relationships should look like. You have to understand that for any relationship to work, you have to put in an equal amount of effort as the other person, whether it is with your family members, spouse, partner, or friends. The best relationships come from people who value each other and are not expecting an unfair amount from the other person. We all thrive in a place of love and consideration.

You also need to be who you really are, and not who you think others want you to be. The truth about who you are, what you do, and what you represent are not things you should consider hiding from a prospective friend or partner. If you allow someone else's preferences to dictate how you act or what you can say, this will not be a good relationship and can become toxic very quickly. Learn to let controlling people go.

Habits to Implement for Achieving Great Social Health

To achieve better social health, you need to work on your mindset and get ready to be a great person for the people around you. A friend in need is a friend indeed.

Know yourself and practice self-care

You cannot help or love people properly if you are not in the right physical and mental state. Self-care is a vital part of that – you need to be able to look after your own needs. Make it a habit to check in with yourself daily; know your mood, your goals, and the things that are on your mind. Self-care includes routine tasks such as cleaning your body, dressing well, getting regular exercise, meditation, and adequate rest. When you look at addressing any issues, remember to include contact with others as a way to alleviate them.

Create energy and time for your relationships

You need to make an effort for your relationships to work. It's a cardinal rule. It can be difficult when you are feeling tired, but you need to set aside time and mental energy for your relationships. Show the people around you that you feel honored and lucky to be with them. You also need to be ready to give and take a lot of emotional support to the people around you. You will often find that this uplifts and energizes you.

Watch the way you criticize people

Nobody is perfect but if you must criticize the people around you, then do it constructively. Do not allow people who depend on you for emotional support to hear you speak ill about them. Jokes that belittle others are seldom well received. Instead, find a more placatory tone to convey what you have observed or noticed about them.

Let me go one step further to break down more of the habits you need for specific relationships in your life.

Habits to develop good family relationships

There are many important aspects to having a healthy family life, and it isn't hard to incorporate them in your day. **Having fun with your family** is important. Families that play together stay together. Go on a picnic or visit a place of mutual interest together. Talk and listen to each other, share experiences and memories. Share opinions and plans; make decisions together. Let everyone have a say.

Rules and boundaries are healthy, and so are schedules. Traditions, after all, are only habits we maintain as a group, and we all know the warmth that comes from them. Things like regular mealtimes and commitments to watching a certain show together at a certain time build a sense of unity. Also, it is important to do chores and exercise together. You are forming habits that support all the golden aspects of life, and teaching them to your children.

Habits to strengthen parent/child relationships

The relationship you build with your children will continue to affect them their whole lives, so even though it will never be perfect, it's important to make it a good one. Show children that you respect and trust them and expect them to make good decisions, and then give them the freedom to learn to do this. Encourage, praise, and reward them when you can, and set rules and boundaries when necessary. Teach them the value of promises – yours and theirs.

Be a part of their lives, and remember to incorporate the five key areas. We all need to learn and work, understand money, take care of our bodies, and connect with others. Children can learn habits that will benefit them for the rest of their lives.

Habits for better spouse/partner relationships

For adults, the spouse/partner is arguably the most important relationship in our lives. Neglecting this relationship inevitably has dire results, but there are countless ways and habits we can develop to care for this relationship. For instance, be open about your feelings; do not avoid or ignore little clashes. Always make sure you resolve problems as soon as possible to prevent resentment from building up. Make your relationship a "no grudges" zone.

Give your partner some space to thrive. Absence makes the heart grow fonder, and clinging will only push people away. Allow your partner some space to meet other people and spend time away from you. It keeps the value of the relationship high. Conversely, ensure that your partner is giving you this space, as well.

Listen to your partner. No matter how tight your schedule is, create time for each other. You can even choose specific times during the week solely for the two of you, such as dining out on a particular day. Your partner needs you to listen to them when they are happy and when they are sad. They may not need advice, but they need you to simply understand them. Pay close attention and listen when they are confiding in you.

Habits to improve friendships

This one is easy: be a dependable friend when needed. Offer encouragement to your friends when they are down or in need of it. Stay in contact; call them to check up on them, set up lunch or dinner dates, share a joke or meme with them, text and show keen interest in their career and personal life. And remember to be appreciative of whatever support has been shown to you. A great friendship works both ways, a friend is someone you feel comfortable supporting and accepting. You have to learn to become vulnerable and truly open up yourself to others if you want a lasting friendship. It is easy to hold a different image of yourself in your business or career but to your family and friends, you should always be true to your colors and embrace the authentic you.

Chapter Summary

Small Habits to Big Changes

No man is an island onto himself. We are all part of a larger, wider network that we need and that can help us grow. It is important that you tap into the benefits that your network of close friends and family members bring to the table. Our connections with other people keep us emotionally and physically healthy and give us the strength to thrive.

Reflection

1. What are the most common things you have been accused of in your relationships? What are the most frequent causes of conflict in your relationships? Can you identify them?
2. What is your tolerance level for nonsense? Do you go hard on anything you cannot tolerate, even from loved ones?
3. Create time for all the relationships that matter to you in life. Relationships need to be nurtured and you must create time and energy to bond with the people you love and care about.

AFTERWORD

Habits are awesome in the way they affect our lives. Nobody is independent of them. They reach farther than our actions or the reasons behind them. They manifest in our actions but are hosted in our nervous system and tightly regulated by hormones. They give color and stability to our lives and offer the major differences in the way we all live. They determine where you can get in life and how smooth the journey is going to be.

For most people, their habits are out of their control. They simply leave their lives on autopilot and allow the winds of fortune to blow them through life. It is no surprise to find such people stuck in a negative feedback loop. They procrastinate about what they should do and lose their discipline. Unable to muster the discipline to move towards their goals, they fail to achieve them. This leads to a pile-up of events that they simply do not have enough time to attend to. Having so much to do on their hands, they procrastinate and leave things in a worse state than they were. This negative feedback loop is one large whirlpool of disappointment, loss of potential,

Afterword

stress, loss of control, and inability to develop. The only way out of it is to build the right habits.

Luckily, this is what this book is about – identifying good and bad habits and learning how to manage them effectively. The message of this book is that you can achieve whatever it is you want to do by correcting your habits. Changing the way you view habits may appear a bit daunting, but just remember that only the beginning of the process will be hard. If you follow the process I have outlined in this book, it will be easier for you to develop the right habits. Once they are fully installed in your brain, you won't even think twice about them.

The right habits will change who you think you are as a person. You will move from "procrastination" to "action." You will no longer miss your exercise routines simply because you won't see them as a chore any longer. You will build better working habits because you love what you are doing, and not because you have to do it. Most importantly, you will have come to understand how implementing habits, you will start to experience massive improvement to your life in these *five golden aspects* (social wellbeing, financial health, physical health, emotional health, and professional development).

I have provided all the information you need to know. However, I would still consider myself a failed teacher if you don't take the proper steps and actions that can change your life. I want you to look back at this moment five, ten years into the future, and be glad you trusted the process.

I need you to understand that you can START making changes in your life NOW. Your current problems are merely manifestations of the bad habits you have developed and the negative feedback loop you have fallen into. Your frustration with finances is not because you are bad with finances; it's because you do not have the right habits for making and

Afterword

managing money. You are not overweight because you are powerless to stop eating junk foods; you are overweight because you failed to implement the right nutritional habits that can help you live better. I know you long for great friendships and relationships; the only way to get them is by building your social health to higher levels by implementing the right habits. In fact, you do not need to be a regular caller at the clinic because of avoidable illnesses; you only need to adjust your lifestyle and make healthy choices that keep you mentally and physically healthy, fit, and strong.

There is only one thing stopping your transformation right now, and that is you. You have the knowledge and the simplest means to becoming the best version of you. You now know what to do and how to do it in the easiest way. That leaves the ball in your court. Will you just sit back and watch bad habits bounce you around the rough edges of life? Or do you care enough to hit back and finally take control of your habits and life?

The choices are clear!

The right habits or bad habits?

A productive routine or a stressful routine?

A better you or the old you?

The difference is all in the habits you choose. Choose wisely!

Act now.

THANK YOU

Reviews are not easy to come by.

As an independent author with a $0 marketing budget, I rely on readers, like you, to leave a short review on Amazon.

Even if it's just a sentence or two!

So if you enjoyed the book, it would mean the world to me if you can leave your feedback in the review section.

I am very appreciative for your review as it truly makes a difference.

Thank you from the bottom of my heart for purchasing this book and reading it to the end!

RESOURCES

Clear, J. (2020). *Atomic Habits*. New York, United States: Penguin Random House.

Cole, S. W., Hawkley, L. C., Arevalo, J. M., & Cacioppo, J. T. (2011). Transcript origin analysis identifies antigen-presenting cells as primary targets of socially regulated gene expression in leukocytes. *Proceedings of the National Academy of Sciences*, 108(7), 3080-3085

Duhigg, C. (2014). *The Power of Habit: Why We Do What We Do in Life and Business*. New York, United States: Penguin Random House.

Fernandez, I. D., Su, H., Winters, P. C., & Liang, H. (2010). Association of Workplace Chronic and Acute Stressors with Employee Weight Status: Data From Worksites in Turmoil. *Journal of Occupational and Environmental Medicine*, 52(Supplement), S34–S41.

Hauge, L. J., Skogstad, A., and Einarsen, S. (2010). The relative impact of workplace bullying as a social stressor at work. *Scandinavian Journal of Psychology*.

Holt-Lunstad, J., Smith, T. B., Baker, M., Harris, T., & Stephenson, D. (2015). Loneliness and social isolation as risk factors for mortality: a meta-analytic review. *Perspectives on psychological science*, 10(2), 227-237.

Meurisse, T. (2016). *Habits That Stick: The Ultimate Guide To Building Powerful Habits That Stick Once and For All*: Independently published.

Schwartz, J. M., & Gladding MD, R. (2012). *You Are Not Your Brain: The 4-Step Solution for Changing Bad Habits, Ending Unhealthy Thinking, and Taking Control of Your Life* (Reprint ed.): Avery.

Printed in Poland
by Amazon Fulfillment
Poland Sp. z o.o., Wrocław

60522241R00073